T0089296

The Little Book of Incredibly
Useful Knots

The Little Book of Incredibly
Useful Knots

200 Practical Knots for Sailors,
Climbers, Campers & Other Adventurers

GEOFFREY BUDWORTH
& JASON DALTON

Library of Congress Cataloging-in-Publication Data
is available on file.

Visit our website at www.skyhorsepublishing.com.

Cover design by Tom Lau
Cover image credit John Fowler

Print ISBN: 978-1-5107-0656-9
Ebook ISBN: 978-1-5107-0657-6

This book was conceived, designed, and produced by
Ivy Press
An imprint of The Quarto Group
The Old Brewery, 6 Blundell Street, London N7 9BH, UK
T (0)20 7700 6700 F (0)20 7700 8066
www.QuartoKnows.com

Creative Director **PETER BRIDGEWATER**
Publisher **SOPHIE COLLINS**
Editorial Director **STEVE LUCK**
Design Manager **TONY SEDDON**
Designer **JANE LANAWAY**
Illustrator **JOHN FOWLER**
Project Editor **MANDY GREENFIELD**

Printed in China

10 9 8 7

PUBLISHER'S NOTE
This book is a general introduction to the usefulness
and pleasure of knotting. Before using any one
of these knots, bends, hitches, etc. in a potentially
hazardous situation—whether at work or at leisure—
with foreseeable risks of injury, damage, or loss, you
are strongly advised to seek the advice and tuition of
suitably qualified practitioners to learn how to tie and
deploy them in such a situation.

KNOT RATINGS
The knots are evaluated under four headings:

5 STRENGTH

5 SECURITY

5 EASE OF TYING

5 EASE OF UNTYING

1 represents the lowest score,
while 5 represents the optimum.

Contents

Introduction

Learn just one helpful knot, use it often, and the cost of this book will be amply repaid. Acquire several knots, and life will never be the same. For, just as being able to cook, garden, swim, read a map, or administer first aid enhances self-reliance and impresses friends, so "knowing the ropes" (being knotwise) is the key to fresh experiences.

Cave dwellers tied the first few knots; a piece of knotted fishing net, found in peat bog in what is today Finland, has been dated to 7,200 BC. Now there are thousands of bends, hitches, lashings, and loops, more than 200 of which are included here. Some have names that still evoke how and by whom they were once tied: the wagoner's hitch, highwayman's hitch, surgeon's knot, and farmer's halter hitch. Bellringers, shopkeepers, linesmen and lumberjacks, trappers and tree surgeons all used a knot or two peculiar to their trades or callings.

Now, whether you engage in demanding outdoor pursuits or need to secure a load to your roof rack, want to tie a bandage or go fishing, there is a knot that will do the job—and this book shows you how. But, as Charles L. Spencer noted in his *Knots, Splices and Fancywork*, "I have found many instances of different names for the same knot . . . and I have had to compromise in some cases."

In this book, knots are grouped loosely according to construction and tying method, and not always according to use. Up-to-date knotting flourishes on the Internet, where numerous web masters represent every kind of knot application, from the basic to the bizarre. In 1990 the New Zealand professor Vaughan Jones was even awarded a Field's Medal (the mathematician's equivalent of a Nobel Prize) for original work in theoretical knotting.

Read on and learn more about the fundamental—yet fascinating—art, craft, and science of knots.

GEOFFREY BUDWORTH

Bends

A bend is the generic term used to describe a knot that joins together two lengths of rope. It should be capable of being untied relatively easily, except when it is tied in fine line. The bends in this section range from the general-purpose (such as the sheet bend) to specialized anglers' knots (such as the mono braid bend and the nail knot).

Square knot

2 2 5 5

The square knot is used to join two lines of the same thickness and material. The knot starts with a simple overhand (*see page 292*), followed by another in reverse. Incorrectly tying this knot will result in a "granny knot," which is much weaker and should be avoided. The square knot will slip if tension is not kept on it, and should be "backed up" (*see page 15*) whenever possible.

Begin by overlaying the two lines (1). Pass the working end once around the other line and bring the ends to the top (2). Then pass the working end once more around the other line, in the opposite direction to the first step (3). An easy way to tie this knot (4) correctly every time is to remember "left over right, right over left" when forming the overhands.

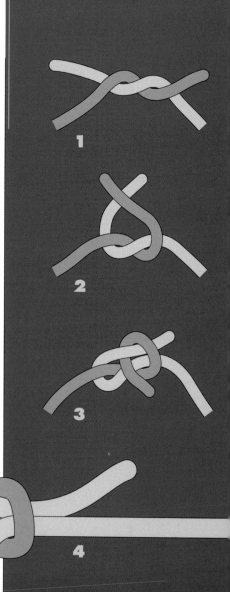

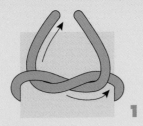

1

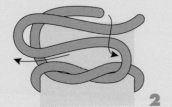

2

3

Slipped square knot

③ ② ④ ⑤

The slipped square knot is generally used when something needs to be secured to a post or spar, but must be capable of being released quickly—for example, to secure netting to an overhead pole for mending, or for lashing to a pole a flag that needs to be unfurled quickly.

Begin by wrapping a length of rope around the post and the item to be secured. Lay the left-hand rope on top of the right, then pass the left end beneath the other rope (1). Now form a bight in the right-hand end, and place it on top of the other rope, passing the free end over the bight and through the loop (2). Pull the working bight and opposite end to tighten the knot (3). The finished knot (4) can be quickly untied by pulling the free end of the bight.

4

Double slipped square knot

Secure shoelaces with this knot—rather than with the double slipped granny knot habitually used by many people—and they are less likely to come inconveniently untied. Also use it in ribbon or pretty string to giftwrap packages.

Tie a half-knot, left over right (1). Make a bight in each end and tie a second half-knot, right over left (2), then pull both loops to tighten the knot (3, 4). Tug either end or both ends to undo it.

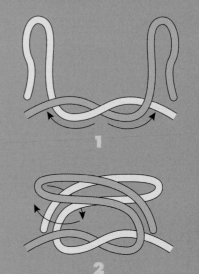

12

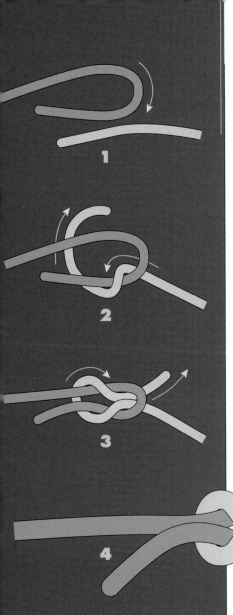

Thief knot

② ① ③ ⑤

This binding knot is superficially identical to the reef or square knot; but, since its short ends emerge on opposite sides, it slips and jams when loaded and so is unreliable. It is a maverick, often used to demonstrate how closely related knots can have distinctly different characters. Tying it, too, is done differently.

Make a bight in one end of the cord (1). Insert the other end up through it, then wrap it around to enclose both legs of the initial bight (2). Tuck it back beside its own standing part (3). To tighten the knot grasp both parts of one cord, both parts of the other cord, and pull in opposite directions.

Overhand bend

This seemingly weak knot, fit only for domestic-quality string and twine, does in fact have a place in the repertoire of climbing knots. It is used during rope retrieval, when it is claimed that it is less likely than some other knots to catch and stick on rocky edges and in crevices. The overhand bend is also reportedly employed on soft sandstone, where jamming metal hardware may be banned, to tie stoppers in short runners and slings. The knot is quick and simple to tie.

In a pair of ends, tie an overhand knot (1, 2). Leave a 6-inch (15-cm) tail in each end (3). Do not use this knot to join ropes of greatly different size or construction.

14

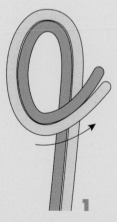

1

2

3

Backing up knots

❸ ④ ❸ ④

Most knots (such as this square knot) will gain considerable security and strength when a simple backup is placed around the standing end, using the working end. A backup should be used whenever large weights or safety are a concern.

You can use a simple overhand knot (*see page 292*) as a backup by passing the working end of a finished knot beneath the standing part and back around to the front; then cross the working end in front and down through the loop you have just created (1, 2). In this way you form an overhand knot (3) that will prevent the end of the main knot from slipping.

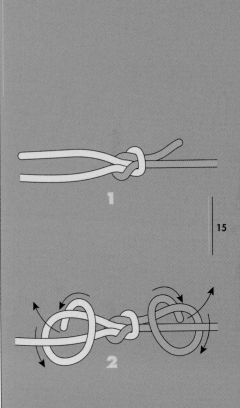

Japanese square knot

This neat and symmetrical two-strand knot can embellish the lanyard holding a knife, whistle, or stopwatch, can secure a fashionable neck scarf, or fasten off a robe's waist tie.

Form a bight in one cord and pass the working end of the other up through it (1). Then pass the cord around the bight to encircle it (2). Pick up the other (so far inactive) end and make a locking tuck (3). Pull evenly, a bit at a time, on each of the four ends in turn to tighten the knot (4).

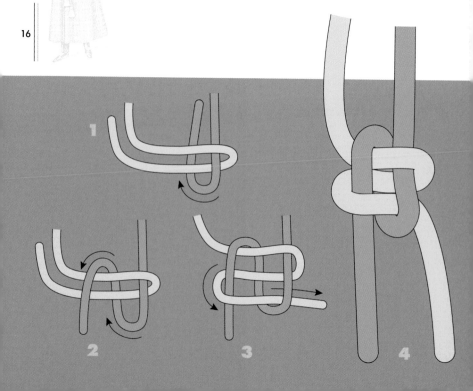

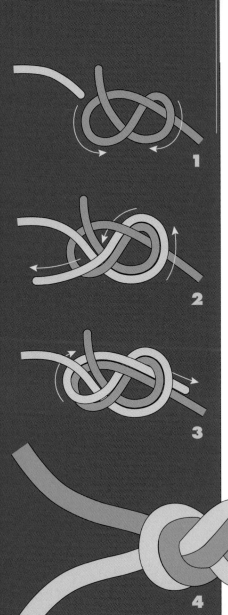

Figure-eight bend

4 **4** **3** **1**

This is a secure knot for joining two lines of equal thickness, but it is difficult to untie it after it has been loaded heavily.

In one working end, make a loop in the line so that the working end emerges above the loop. Wrap the working end around and under the standing part so that you can feed the end through the loop you have created, from above to below (1). With the other line, retrace the figure eight, following the same path in the opposite direction (2). Now retrace the lead of both strands, removing unwanted twists (3). Turn the work over to check that all ugly crossings (which could weaken the knot) have been eliminated, and the ends will be seen to emerge on opposite sides of the knot (4). Pull it tight.

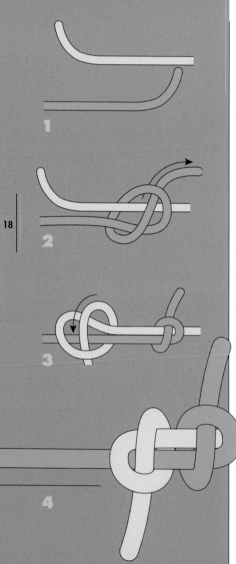

Fisherman's knot

3 4 3 1

The fisherman's knot joins
two lines in a secure bend.
The single fisherman's knot
shown here is useful for
small lines and will hold in
slippery material, such as
monofilament line.

Start by overlaying
the two lines so that
the working ends face
in opposite directions
(1). Make a small loop
in the nearest line and
take it around the
second line, then pass
the working end
through the loop to
form an overhand
(2). Repeat the
process with the
second line, tying it
around the first line
(3); it is useful to turn
the entire working
around after the first
overhand to ensure
that you tie identical
parts. When tied
correctly, the standing
ends can be pulled so
that the two overhands
slide together and
mesh neatly (4).

Double fisherman's knot

⑤ ⑤ ③ ①

The double fisherman's knot is a stronger version of the fisherman's bend and has less tendency to slip. This knot and a triple-wrap version are commonly used in mountaineering and rock climbing.

Begin with the two working ends overlaying each other and facing in opposite directions (1). In your right hand take the working end that is pointing away from you. Wrap it twice around the other line, making an X on the rope. Then feed the working end through the wraps beneath the X and pull tight (2). Rotate your work so that you can repeat the procedure with the opposite line (3). Pull the standing ends away from each other to draw the knots together (4). A proper double fisherman's knot will have the two knots meshing closely, with the Xs on the same side.

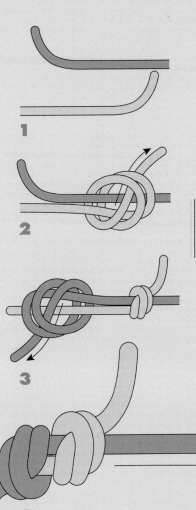

19

Water knot

This knot is typically tied in the flat webbing used by climbers and mountaineers. Because of this, it is sometimes known as a tape knot. The water knot is an overhand follow-through and is simple to tie. Although it makes a very solid knot for webbing, it is difficult to untie after it has been loaded.

Start by making a simple overhand in one working end (1). Take the end of the second line through the overhand, retracing the original path in the opposite direction (2). Continue following the original path with the second line until the overhand has been completed (3). Make sure that all the lines are laid neatly next to each other and, if you are using webbing, that there are no folds or twists in the knot. There should be plenty of extra line at the working ends after the knot is completed (4).

1

2

3

4

21

One-way knot ❸ ❸ ❷ ❷

The one-way knot gets its name from the fact that the working ends face in the same direction when the knot is finished. It is therefore useful in joining two lines where the knot must pass through an eye, hook, or pulley, since it can travel in one direction without getting hung up.

Begin by forming a loop in the end of the line that goes to the pulley (1). Bring the working end behind the standing part (2), and feed it through the loop you have just made (3). With the other line, begin retracing the knot by inserting it beside the working end of the first half of the knot (4). Then pass this line around the standing line, keeping on the same side of the rope. Finish by feeding the working end through from bottom to top (5), leaving several inches of line past the knot. Draw the knot up to tighten it, as shown turned over (6).

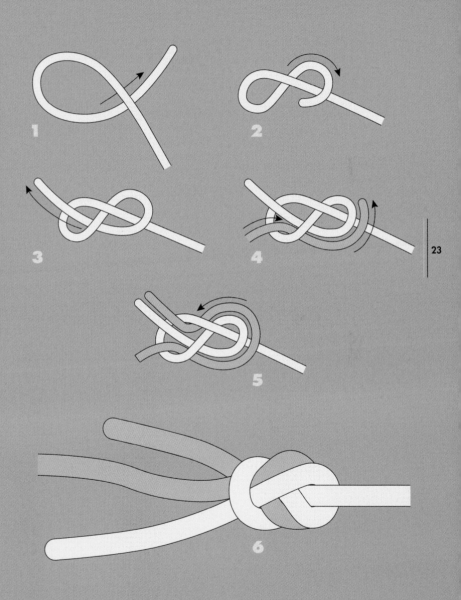

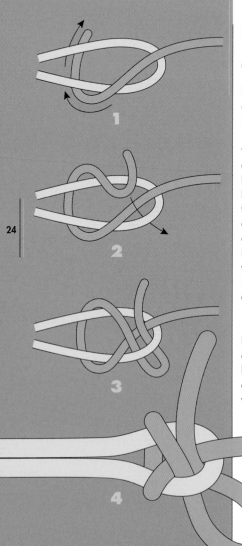

Lapp knot

③ ③ ④ ⑤

Knots often work best when combined. Tie an angler's (perfection) loop (*see pages 110–111*) in one end of a waist tie, and the ideal companion to it will be the Lapp knot, so called because Lapps have been seen to tether reindeer with it. Not only does it have a slipknot or drawloop, but, when this is tugged, the knot falls apart without further fiddling (unlike many other so-called quick-release knots).

Lay the unknotted end on top of the loop made by the angler's loop (1), wrap it around (2), and tuck a bight over itself and down through the loop (3). Pull the end (4) to release the knot.

24

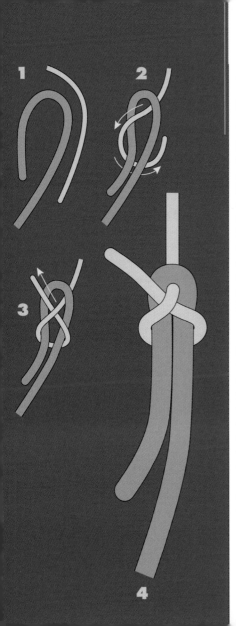

Sheet bend

❶ ② ④ ⑤

This is a very old knot, used to join two lines of different thicknesses. It is quick to tie and is commonly used when hauling a large rigging line with a smaller "tag" line. In practice this knot can easily slip if the line diameters are very different, or if the material itself is very slippery (such as polypropylene rope). In that case there are several other knots that may be used for this purpose.

Begin the knot with the larger line, making a bight with the ends facing to the left (1). Insert the working end of the smaller line up through the bight from the bottom. Pass the end around the back of bight from left to right (2). Finally, lay the second working end above the bight, but beneath the small line (3). The working ends of both the large and the small rope should always emerge from the knot on the same side. Tighten by pulling on the bight and the standing end of the small line (4).

Slipped sheet bend

❸ ❸ ❹ ❺

All knots depend for their
holding power on a combination
of friction and nip, both of which
are minimal (although adequate)
in the common sheet bend.
This quick-release version may,
curiously, increase both nip and
friction somewhat, because the
knot is fattened by the insertion
of an extra knot part and
added crossing points.

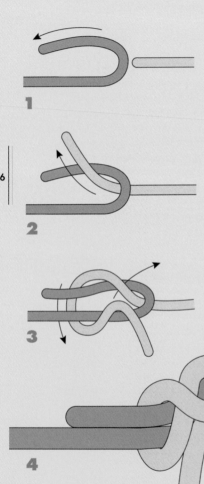

Begin as if tying
a basic sheet
bend (*see page 25*),
making a bight in the
larger line with the
ends facing to the left
(1). Insert the working
end of the smaller
line up through the
bight from the
bottom (2).

Pass the end around
the back of bight
from left to right (3).
Do not pull the
working end
completely through
beneath its own
standing part, but
make a drawloop,
before tightening
the knot (4).

Double sheet bend

●●●●

When a sheet bend (*see page 25*) cannot cope with two lines of somewhat dissimilar thickness or stiffness, this reinforced version may do the trick.

Make a bight in the larger line, with the ends facing to the left. Insert the working end of the smaller line up through the bight from the bottom, then pass it around the back (1) and over the bight, but beneath the small line (2). Ensure that both short ends are on the same side of the knot, then tuck the working end around a second time and beneath the standing part (3). Pull on both ends to tighten the knot (4).

Racking bend

5 4 4 5

Use this bend to join a thin or flexible rope to a heavier or stiffer one, which might otherwise tend to capsize and spill the lighter line.

Make a bight in the weightier or stiffer rope. Pass the working end of the lighter line through the bight (1) and commence a series of figure-eight "racking" turns, weaving in and out of the bight (2). Pull each turn snugly tight before going on to the next. Finish by tucking the end beneath a convenient part of itself (3) and pulling the knot up tight (4).

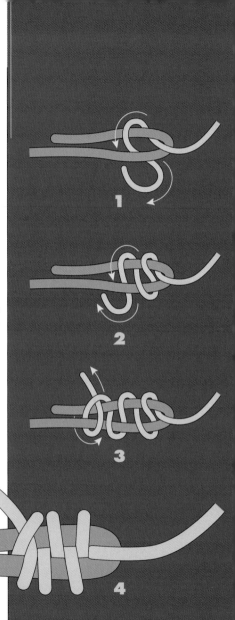

Adjustable bend

⑤⑤③③

This slide-and-grip knot was devised by climbing guide Robert Chisnall of Ontario, Canada, in 1982. It will join two ropes, cords, or lengths of webbing (tape), and in both ends of the same stuff can create a sling or strop. Each one of the twin knots in the bend may be shifted by hand in either direction.

Hold the two ropes, cords, or webbing together and parallel, with the ends facing in opposite directions. Wrap one end twice around the adjacent standing part (1) and then tuck the end around both bits of rope and beneath the second turn (2). Reverse the half-completed knot end-for-end, then repeat the process with the other working end (3). Tighten both knots before use (4).

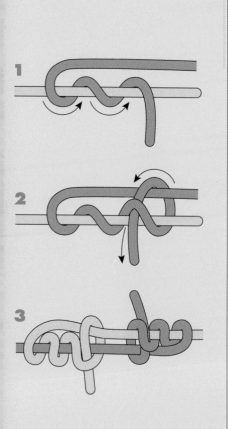

Seizing bend

This is an alternative to the racking bend (*see page 28*) and a trifle easier to tie. It was devised and first published in 1986 by retired research scientist and inventor Dr. Harry Asher.

Make a bight in the larger or stiffer of two dissimilar lines, and take a turn around it with the smaller or more manageable one (1). Allow a couple of inches (about 5–6 cm) and begin a series of tight, wrapping turns with the working end back toward the tip of the bight (2, 3). Then pull out the initial round turn and pass the resulting loop over the short end of the bight (4). Work the knot tight and, for extra security, tie the working end to its own standing part with a bowline (*see page 63*) (5).

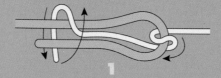

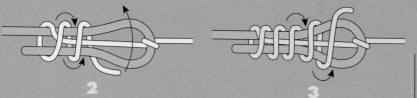

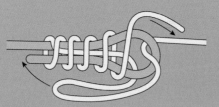

Carrick bend   ❷ ❷ ❸ ❹

The name carrick bend first appeared in the eighteenth century. This basic knot has many applications both on land and at sea, but is a weaker knot than some, due to the many tight curves to which the rope is subjected under weight. However, it does not readily slip under strain and will be secure and lasting for loads weighing half the breaking strength of the line.

Begin with a bight in the end of one line, with the working and standing ends crossed. Lay the working end of the second line beneath the loop in the first line (1). Cross the second line over the opposite standing end, under the opposite working end, then back over the loop. Then cross under the same line and over the next loop (2). Notice that the crossings alternate over and under. Pull all four lines emerging from the knot (3). Then pull just the standing parts to tighten (4).

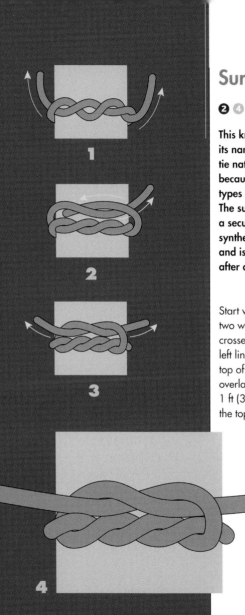

Surgeon's knot

2 4 3 4

This knot may have gotten its name from being used to tie natural suture material, because it is secure in many types of natural rope. The surgeon's knot forms a secure bend in today's synthetic materials as well, and is fairly easy to untie after a load.

Start with the two working ends crossed, with the left line placed on top of the right and overlapped by about 1 ft (30 cm). Bring the top line beneath the other with two complete wraps (1). Cross the working ends again, this time with the right side over the left (2). Bring the top line beneath and around the other with one wrap (3). Pull mainly on the standing ends to tighten (4).

Albright knot ❺ ❹ ❸ ❶

The Albright is used to tie a small monofilament leader to a larger-diameter fishing or fly-casting line. It is effective even when attaching monofilament to nylon-coated wire, because it grips very tightly. As with most fishing knots, you should not bother to untie it from monofilament line, but simply clip the knot off and retie.

Take a bight in the larger-diameter line, then run the smaller line through it (1). Begin wrapping the working end of the smaller line around the bend and the standing end (2). Continue for many wraps—at least six. Feed the working end around the standing part and through the end of the bight in the larger line (3). Then pull the working end and cinch the wraps so that they lie perfectly alongside one another (4). Moisten and pull tight along the standing ends (5). Trim the excess off the smaller line to finish (6).

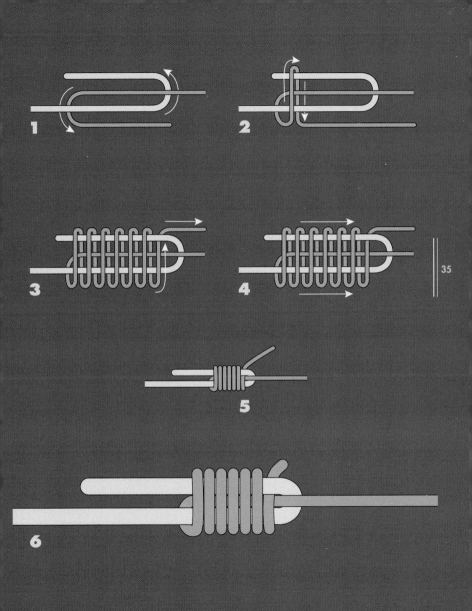

35

Zeppelin bend

Pioneering German airships were named after their designer, Count Ferdinand von Zeppelin. The bow mooring line of one such 1930s craft—the US Navy-owned and -operated *Los Angeles*—is said to have been made fast to the ground mooring rope with this knot (and no other) on the orders of her captain, Lieutenant-Commander Charles Rosendahl. For this reason the knot is also known as the Rosendahl knot or bend. It is equally reliable in all kinds of modern cordage and usage.

Grasp both ropes or cords in one hand with the ends drooping to the right (in this instance) (1). Lead the frontmost working end around both standing parts and tuck it through from back to front, tying a simple overhand in itself (2). Bring the standing part of the other line across to the right, in front of its own short end (3). Tuck that short end over two and under two knot parts (4). The resulting knot consists of two interlocked overhand knots. Pull on both ends to tighten (5).

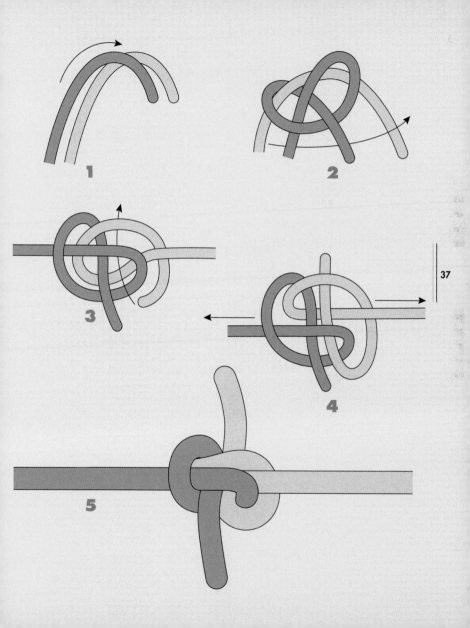

1

2

3

4

5

37

Hunter's bend

Hunter's bend (named after Dr. Edward Hunter, but also known as the rigger's bend) is a very secure knot that takes a little practice to tie quickly, but forms a secure knot when complete.

Start with two ends of rope overlapped by about 1 ft (30 cm) (1). Form a loop in one end, and mirror it with the other end, so that they lie against each other, facing in opposite directions (2). Each free end should then be passed around the loop from the outside of the knot, then through the loop itself. The two ends will pass through the loops in opposite directions (3). Pull outward on the standing parts and work the knot to tighten (4). The remaining working ends can be trimmed close to the knot if necessary (5).

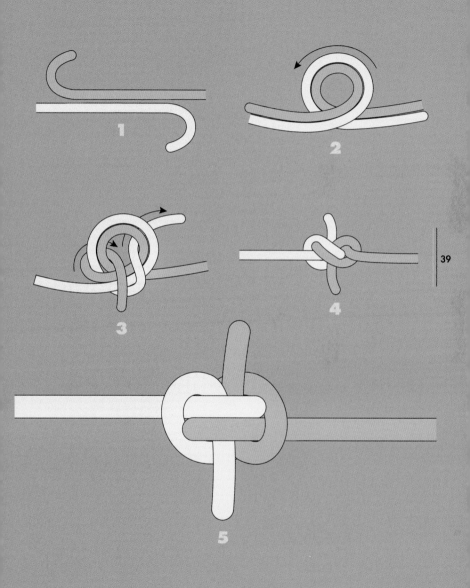

Blood knot

This is an old fishing knot used for joining small monofilaments together. Fishermen join lengths of progressively smaller line with it to create a fly-casting leader. It can be used on most freshwater monofilaments and is strong, as long as care is taken to moisten and carefully tighten the lines. Tightening them too quickly can, however, weaken the lines.

Start with the two ends of the lines overlapped by about 1 ft (30 cm) (1). With both lines, make at least eight full wraps around the other (2). Pull apart the wraps at the middle, creating an "eye," then bring the working ends back through the eye in opposite directions (3). Moisten the knot and pull the working ends apart while cinching up the knot (4). Trim the excess line off close to the knot (5).

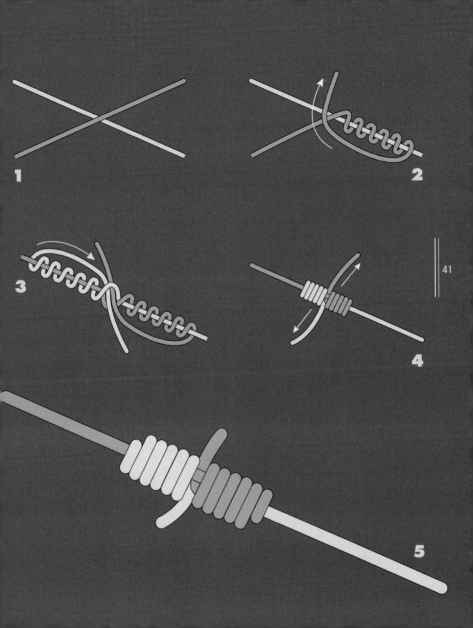

Mono braid bend

④ ④ ❸ ❶

This heavy-duty knot will join dissimilar angling lines, braid-to-monofilament, and so on.

Tie a Bimini twist (*see pages 122–123*) in the lighter or more flexible of the two lines (1), then wrap it twice around the other line (2). Take the second line at least six times around its opponent, before tucking the tag end back through the remaining bight (3, 4). Tug the arrangement snug and tight (5). Cut off the end close to the knot.

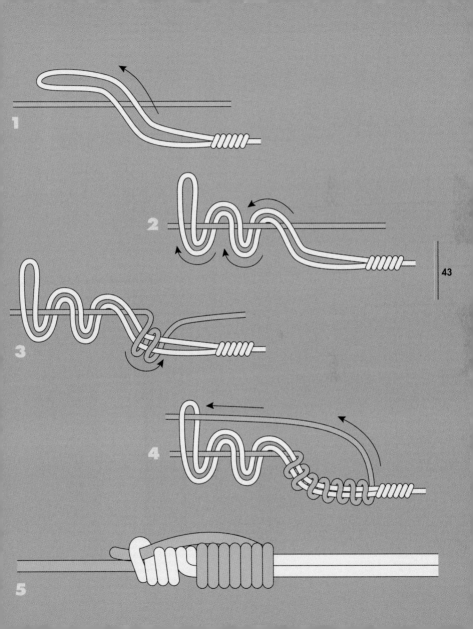

Double grinner knot ❺ ❺ ❸ ❶

You can join two lines of similar size, weight, or strength together with two identical knots which, back-to-back, slide together. Each of these versatile knots is more widely known, however, as a uni (universal) knot, because, its fans claim, it can also be made into a loop or a snell to hook and lure.

Bring together the two lines to be joined, parallel, with the working ends pointing in opposite directions. Create a loop with one end (1), then tuck four wrapping turns through it (2) and tighten (3). Turn the work end-for-end and repeat the process (4, 5). Pull on the standing part of both lines to unite the twin knots (6).

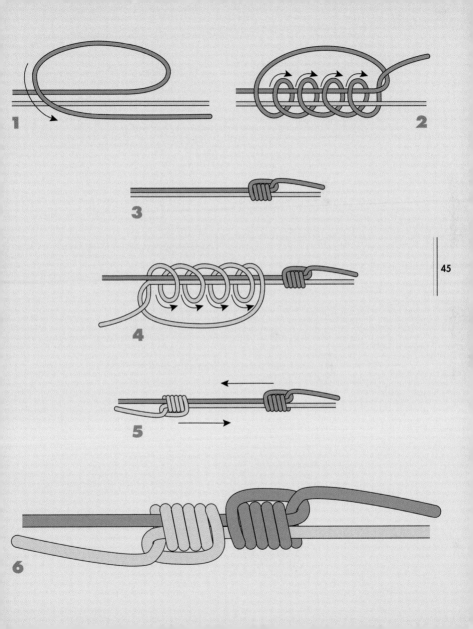

Butterfly bend

A lot of loop knots can be converted into bends. This adaptation of the alpine butterfly loop (*see pages 90–91*) seems to have emerged, in 1975, from the brain and hands of American master rigger Brion Toss, who originally called it the Strait bend (after the Strait of Juan de Fuca in the Pacific Northwest). It is strong and secure, neither slipping nor jamming.

Form two interlocked loops of opposite handedness (that is, where the two entwined parts spiral in opposite directions), exactly as shown (1). Bring each working end in turn to the front of the knot and tuck it down through the central space common to both loops (2, 3). Tighten the couple of interlaced overhand knots that are the result (4, 5).

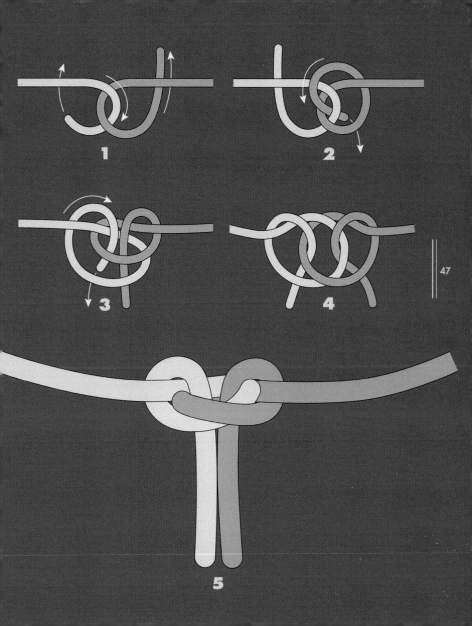

Nail knot | ❹ ❸ ❸ ❶

The nail knot is an adaptation of snelling (*see pages 222–223*) and is used in fly-fishing to join the fly line to the butt section of the leader. Its name is said to have originated in the 1950s when a noted American fly-fisherman named Joe Brooks learned the knot in Argentina using a horseshoe nail.

Place a doubled length of the thinner line alongside the thicker one and, prior to tying, add a nail (although a drinking straw, or the hollow case of a ballpoint pen, works even better) (1). With the working end of the fly line, make between six and eight turns around both leader and nail (or tube) and its own standing part (2). Next, pass the working end back through the space preserved by the nail (or inside the tube) (3); when the end emerges, withdraw the nail (or tube) (4). Remove all unwanted slack from the wrapping turns, and pull both working end and standing part in opposite directions to tighten them (5). Finally, snip off the tag end close to where it protrudes from the knot (6).

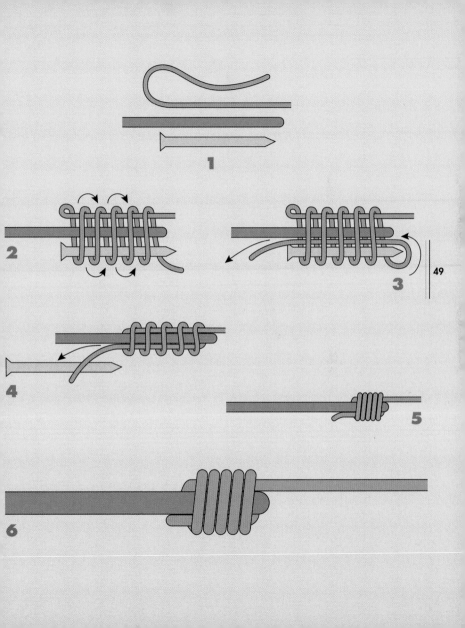

Needle knot   ❺ ❺ ❸ ❶

More streamlined than the preceding nail knot, this is another way to attach a fly line to a monofilament leader; and, because the thinner line is actually inserted into the thicker one, it is also more secure.

Thread the fly line onto a needle, insert the needle into the end of the leader (1), and force it out through the side (2); alternatively, heat the needle and make a hole, then push the fly line (end carefully pointed with a razor blade) through after it. Make a series of wrapping turns (3, 4), using the needle in the same way as you did the nail when tying the nail knot (*see pages 48–49*). Tuck the end through the space created by the needle (5). Tighten the knot and snip the tag end off close to it (6).

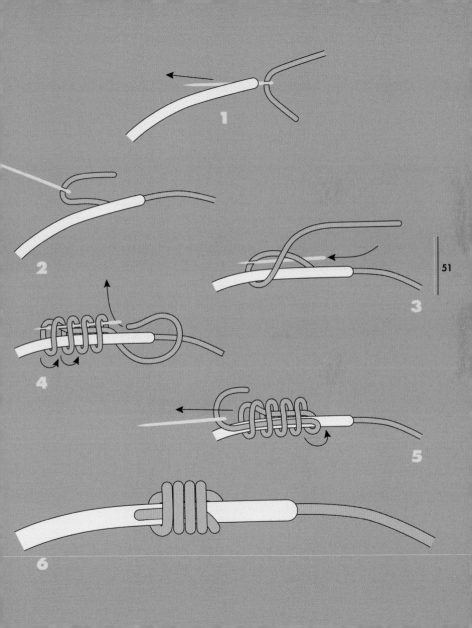

51

Vice versa

Innovative British knot tier Harry Asher devised this bend to join slimy or slippery lengths of rope or cord that are of similar diameter and construction. It will even cling to shock elastics (bungee cord), which shed many otherwise trustworthy knots. The vice versa is a comparative newcomer to the knotting scene, having first been published in 1989.

Lay the two lines to be joined parallel and close together. Wrap one end around the opposing standing part (1), then repeat the process with other end (2, 3), and cross the ends (4). Tuck each end through the end loop beside its own standing part (5). Work the knot snug by pulling a bit at a time on each working end and standing part in turn (6).

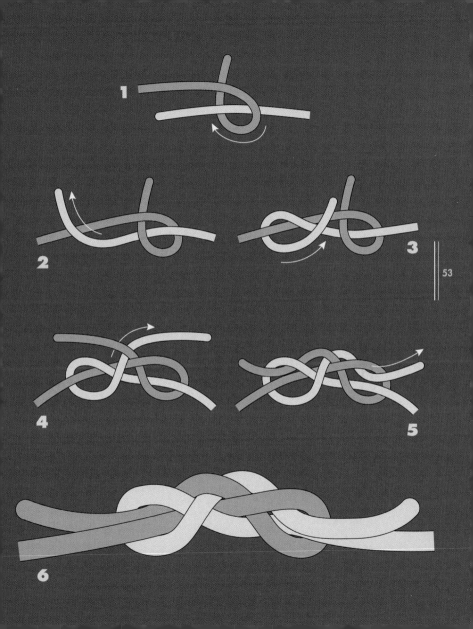

Simple Simon (double)   ❹ ❹ ❹ ❹

This—like the vice versa (*see pages 52–53*)—is another new knot, less than 20 years old, from the brain and fingers of Harry Asher. It is intended to join two ropes or cords of somewhat dissimilar diameter or construction.

Form a bight in the larger or stiffer of the two lines and pass the other working end through it (1). Wrap the end of the lighter line up around the front, down the back (2), and up around the front once more (3). Then make a return journey, going over at each crossing point (4), and tucking the working end up beside its own standing part (5). Pull on both legs or on each line to tighten (6).

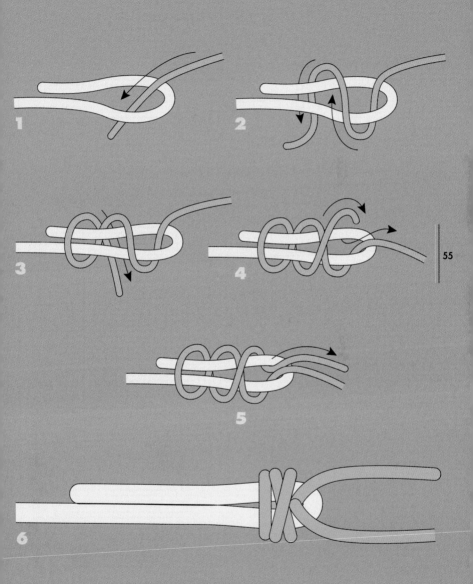

55

Twin bowline bend

This heavy-duty bend can be employed to join together a couple of thick and less flexible ropes or cables, such as towlines, whether on land or afloat. First, learn the common bowline (*see page 63*); then this adaptation will be easier to tie.

Lay the two lines together, parallel and pointing in opposite directions. Create a loop in the standing part of one line and pass the working end of the other line up through it (1). Then pass it around behind the standing part, and back down beside itself (2). Turn the work end-for-end and repeat the process (3, 4, 5). Tighten each knot in turn by tugging the standing and working ends away from one another (6).

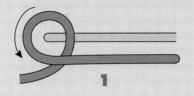

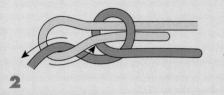

1

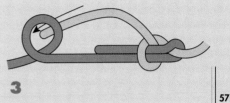

3

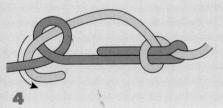

2

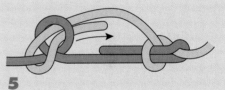

5

4

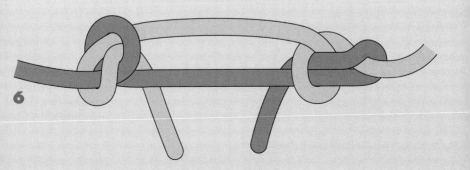

6

Loops

Loops are often employed as hitches, or they may be used in climbing, caving, and rescue operations to create a fixed loop or loops (as in the many variations on the bowline). Other loops offer a slide-and-grip function (for instance, the Tarbuck knot), a noose effect (the tucked double overhand loop), or a loop at the end of fishing line (the Bimini twist).

Overhand loop ❸ ⑤ ⑤ ❷

Most suitable for thread, twine, and string, because it is difficult to untie once tightly tied, this quick and easy fixed loop may be used sparingly in larger cordage and rope if it is not to be heavily loaded.

Make a bight in the end of the line (1), then simply tie it in an overhand knot (2, 3). Take care to eliminate unnecessary and undesirable twists before tightening the knot (4), since a messy knot is often a weak one, while a neat finish retains the inherent strength of knot and line.

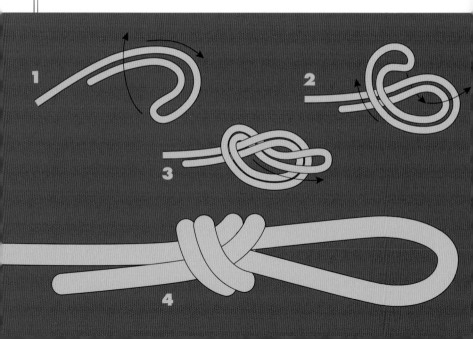

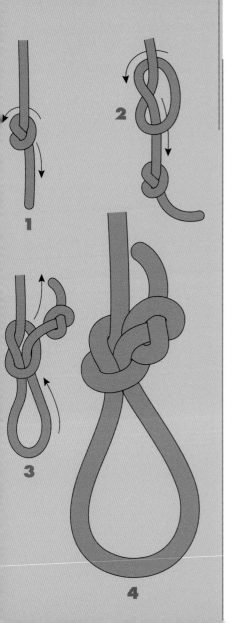

Stopped loop

② ④ ④ ⑤

Basic, even primitive, this loop knot is suitable for coarse string and odd jobs in the garage, workshop, and kitchen, but should not be employed for more demanding outdoor pursuits or sporting purposes.

Tie a simple overhand (*see page 292*) close to the working end (1), then tie another at a distance from the first that is twice as far as the intended final length of the loop required (2). Tuck the knotted end through this second knot so that it lies alongside its own standing part (3). Pull everything tight to finish the stopped loop (4).

Reef-knotted loop

● ○ ● ●

A neat accessory to a waist
tie that incorporates a Lapp
knot (*see page 24*) is this
loop, into which workers
of all kinds might slip a
hammer, wrench, or other
tool. It is another example
of combining knots for
added effectiveness.

Create a downward tongue
or bight, and with the two
working ends tie a half-
knot so that it passes on
either side of the bight
(1, 2). Add a second
half-knot of opposite
handedness (that is,
one in which the two
entwined parts spiral in
the opposite direction)
(3), and pull it tight (4).

1

2

3

4

Bowline

The bowline is an ancient knot with a rich history. The name comes from the lines used to attach the furls of sails to the bow for stabilization. But the knot is probably much older than that, because similar knots are found in prehistoric records. Current uses for the bowline include temporary moorings for small craft, several rescue applications, and whenever a fixed loop is needed that will not close around a waist, leg, or foot.

Start the knot by forming a bight of rope, with the working end on the right. In the standing end form a loop, with the remaining part of the standing end leading from beneath the loop (1). Insert the working end through the loop from underneath (2). Bring the working end behind the standing line from right to left and back down through the loop (3). Tighten by pulling down on the large loop created by the knot (4).

1 **2** **3** **4**

One-handed bowline

Having learned to tie a bowline whatever way comes easiest, it is helpful to master this one-handed method. A time-honored exhortation to all those working afloat, up trees, or in any other precarious position is "Use one hand for the job, but keep the other for yourself." In other words, hold on. This technique is for those situations.

Make a loop of the required size, crossing the end over its standing part (1). Then, with a rolling action of hand and wrist, tuck the working end down, around, and up through the large loop; this action creates a smaller loop (2). Still gripping the end, slip the hand up through this secondary loop (3), pass the working end around the standing part, and pull it back down through the small loop (4, 5). For extra security, tie the end to the nearest loop leg with an overhand knot (6).

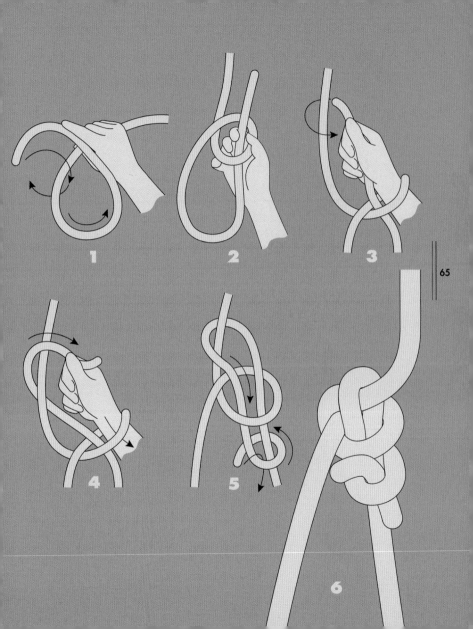

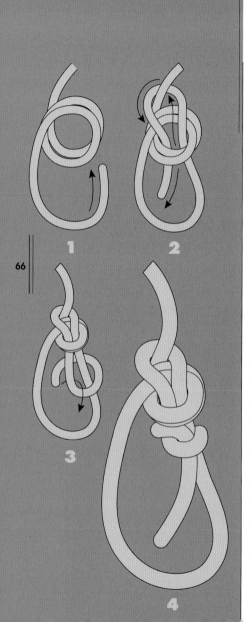

Double bowline

5 **4** **2** **3**

When there is danger of a simple bowline knot coming untied due to abrasion or motion of the knot, then a double bowline is more secure.

Begin by forming two loops in the working end of the line, leaving enough working end to complete the rest of the knot. Each loop should be made with the standing line emerging from underneath, and the second loop should lie on top of the first without being twisted or flipped in any way (1). Feed the working end up through the loops from the bottom. Pass it behind the standing line, then feed it back down through the loops so that the end is within the large loop (2). Pull on the working ends to tighten. For extra security, the knot can be backed up by first passing the remaining working end around the adjacent part of the large loop (3), then feeding it down through the loop just created, to form an overhand around that section (4).

Running bowline

The bowline is used to create a fixed loop that will not slide. When a situation arises where you need a loop that will slide, you can make a running bowline. This knot is used for snares and traps, as well as any time that a secure attachment is needed that will remain under a load.

Start by making a standard bowline knot (*see page 63*). Then run the standing end through the main loop of the bowline (1). This enables the bowline to be moved up and down the rope (2).

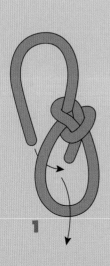

1

2

This knot creates two fixed loops in the end of a line. It gives more strength and security than a single bowline, and is used by some climbers as a tie-in point on a rope.

Begin with a large bight at the end of a rope. Make a loop above the bight, with the standing line coming from the bottom of the loop (1). Pass the free end of the bight up through the loop (2). Pass the free loop around the entire knot (3), then pull down on the double loop (4).

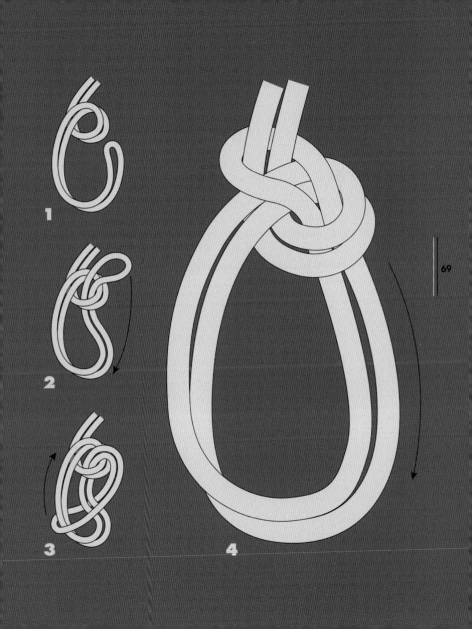

1

2

3

4

69

Overhand shortening

There are two principal uses for this contrivance: learn one, get one free. It is an effective shortening, tied in the bight, of any rope or webbing that is overlong for the job in hand; and it may also be used to create a pair of fixed leg loops for a climbing harness.

Form an S-shape in the material to be tied (1) and press it together, taking care to keep the tape or webbing flat and untwisted throughout (2). Tie an overhand knot in the triple thickness, once more ensuring that no unwanted twist occurs (3, 4). Pull everything snug and tight (5).

70

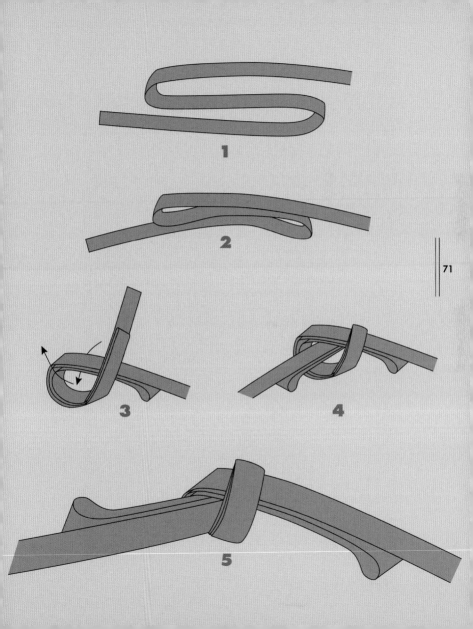

1

2

3

4

5

Triple loop bowline

Learn the common bowline (*see page 63*), then this version with three loops is easily tied. Each loop can be adjusted to a different size, although it takes time and patience to do so; then the knot can be used as an improvised chair sling for emergency rescues, or as a routine multipoint anchorage for all kinds of boating, climbing, and pioneering activities.

Make a long bight in one end of the rope (1) and then, treating the doubled portion as it if were a single line (2), form a small loop (3). Now tuck the working of the bight up through the loop, from back to front (4), leaving sufficient slack to create large twin loops, and pass it from right to left behind the twin standing parts of the line (5). Finally, tuck the working end of the bight back down through the loop to act as the third loop (6).

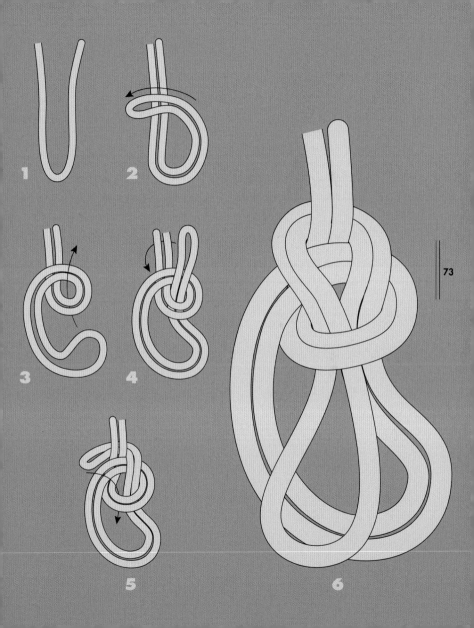

Slipped bowline

❸ ❸ ❹ ❹

The common bowline is a tried-and-trusted knot, much used by all who have to make rope work for them; although it is not especially strong or secure, it can sometimes jam and be hard to undo. So if it is to be tied in coarse cordage and then heavily loaded, consider using this slipped version.

Pass the working end up through the loop (1), and around behind the standing part of the line (2), as if tying a basic bowline (*see page 63*), but then tuck a bight (not the end) down through beside the adjacent loop leg (3). Tighten the knot around this bight (4). To release the knot, simply tug the end to remove the drawloop.

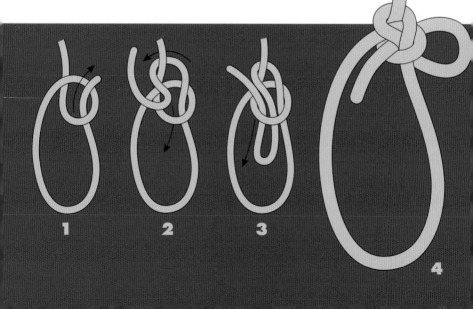

1   **2**   **3**   **4**

Tucked bowline ④ ④ ④ ④

This adaptation of a triple-loop bowline was first proposed by Robert Chisnall in the mid-1980s, as an aid to teaching. The adjacent twin loops can be used by a climbing instructor and trainee, while the back-tucked third loop is belayed to a convenient tree or other anchorage.

In a long bight, tie a triple bowline; treating the doubled portion as it if were a single line, form a small loop (1). Now tuck the working of the bight up through the loop, behind the twin standing parts of the line, and back down through the loop to act as the third loop (2). Then tuck the third loop around and back through alongside the working end and standing part of the rope (3).

1

2

3

Portuguese bowline

❸ ❸ ❹ ❹

Knowing the common bowline (*see page 63*) makes this twin-loop version easier to tie. The loops are adjustable to some extent, although as one is enlarged, the other shrinks.

Make a loop (with the working end uppermost) in the standing part of the rope, and then pass the end through the loop from back to front (1). Take a second similar pass and go around behind the standing part (2). Tuck the end back down beside itself (3, 4). Then pull to tighten the knot (5).

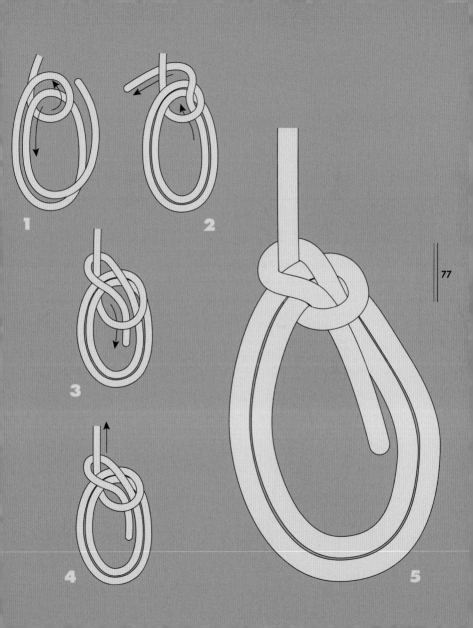

1

2

3

4

5

Spanish bowline

This is a classic twin forked-loop knot from the days of sail, when it was used to improvise a rope chair to hoist crewmen aloft, or to suspend them over the side on ladder staging. It is tied (and untied) in the bight—that is, without the need to use either end of the rope or cord. With practice it is easier to tie than it looks; but, as with all knots, make one wrong twist or tuck and something else (or no knot at all) will result.

Locate the middle of the line and bend a bight backward down behind the twin standing parts to form a couple of loops (1). Twist the left loop clockwise and the right loop counterclockwise (2). Then pass the left-hand loop up through its right-hand partner, from back to front (3). Taking hold of both sides of the large lower loop, pull a bight from front to back through each of the smaller upper loops (4), and then tighten the knot (5).

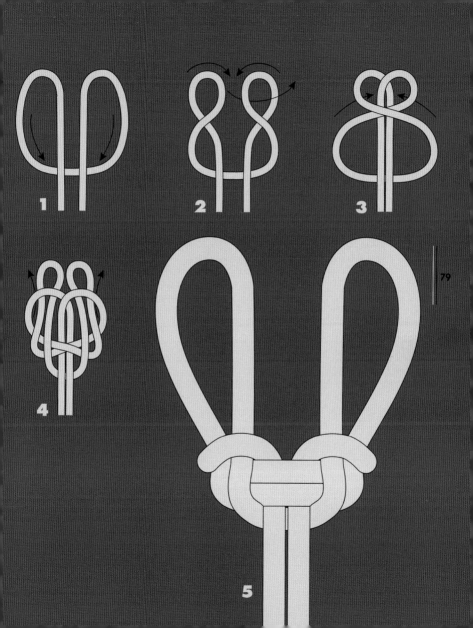

Carrick loop

Knowing the start of a common bowline (*see page 63*) will make tying this fixed-loop knot easier.

Make a loop with the working end on top (1). Then pass the end up through the loop from back to front and lead it behind its own standing part, from right to left (2). Bring the end around in front of the left-hand leg of the loop and tuck it under-under-over up through the knot (3). Pull on both ends to tighten (4).

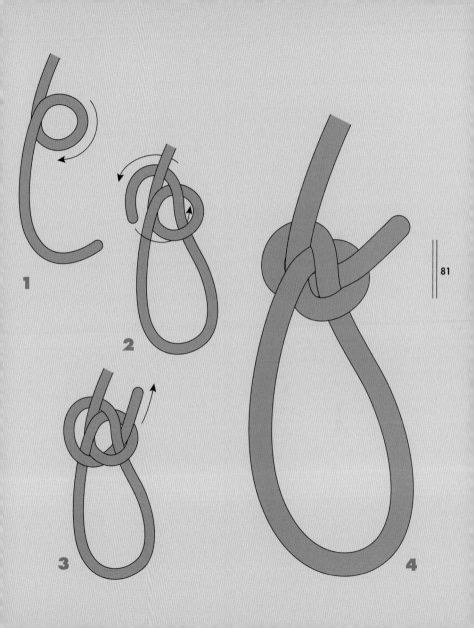

1

2

3

4

81

Surgeon's loop

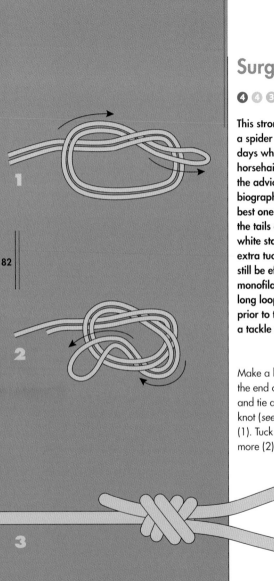

4 4 3 1

This strong knot (also called a spider loop) hails from the days when anglers still used horsehair lines and believed the advice of the Greek biographer Plutarch that the best ones were made from the tails of thoroughbred white stallions. With an extra tuck or two it can still be effective in nylon monofilaments to make a long loop in fishing lines prior to the assembly of a tackle rig.

Make a long bight in the end of the line and tie an overhand knot (*see page 292*) (1). Tuck at least once more (2), then pull the loop away from the remainder of the line to tighten (3). In thinner, slicker lines, add more tucks. Snip the end off short.

82

Tarbuck knot

British climber and skier Ken Tarbuck devised this adjustable loop knot in 1952 for use in the new nylon climbing ropes; but it proved to be damaging to the more hi-tech kernmantel (core-and-sheath) ropes that superseded them, so it was discarded. It remains an effective slide-and-grip loop, however, to tighten and slacken off such diverse, general-purpose cordage applications as tent guy-lines or clotheslines.

This knot must be wrapped and tucked just so. With the working end, take two full turns around the standing part to form a loop (1). Bring the end up at the front of the knot (2), and pass it around the back of the standing part, before tucking it over and then under itself (3). Methodically tighten all parts of the knot (4). Unloaded, it can be slid along to increase or decrease the size of the loop; loaded, it locks up.

83

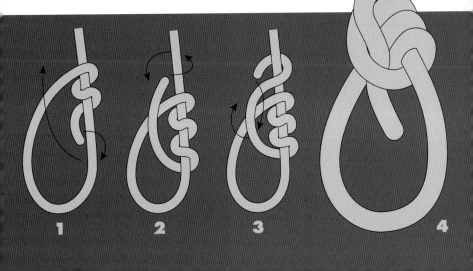

1   **2**   **3**   **4**

Handcuff knot

🅸 🅸 🅸 🅸

This multipurpose knot can be used to make a temporary fireman's rescue chair knot, to hobble live animals so that they do not stray, or even to sling dead carcasses to enable them to be carried.

Throw a couple of loops (one overhand, the other underhand) and overlap them (1). Draw the right-hand one down through the left, and the left-hand one up through the right (2). Pull the loops in opposite directions to tighten the knot (3); pull one or both of the ends to adjust the size of the loops.

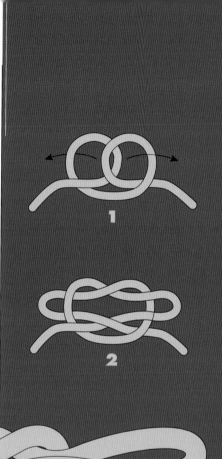

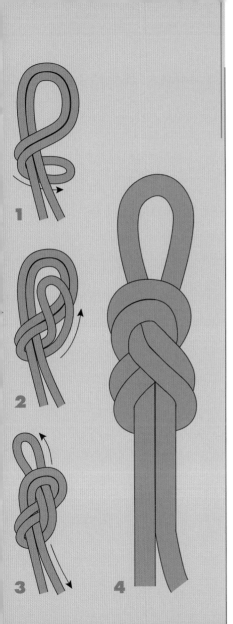

Figure-eight loop

5 **5** **4** **2**

This knot creates a strong loop at the end of a rope. It is used extensively in climbing, caving, and rescue operations, because it is easy to learn and to inspect visually. The only drawback is that it binds tightly under heavy loads and takes some effort to untie.

Start with a bight at the end of the rope to make a loop. Wrap the working end of the loop around the standing part from front to back (1). Bring the working end back around to the front before feeding it through the loop you have created (2). Pull the loop away from the standing line to tighten (3). Contouring of the knot so that the lines are even and parallel will create the strongest knot (4) and will make it easier to untie.

Double figure-eight loop

Akin to the bowline on a bight (*see pages 68–69*), this knot is preferred by some people for climbing, caving, and other outdoor pursuits, because they reason that tying a figure eight is less likely to go wrong.

Take a long bight of rope and form it into a figure-eight knot outline (1). Next, hook and partially pull through the lower half of the figure eight a doubled bight (that is, four sections of rope) (2). Bring the single bight down the front of the almost-completed knot (3), lift the twin bights through it from back to front, and replace the single bight at the top and rear of the knot (4, 5).

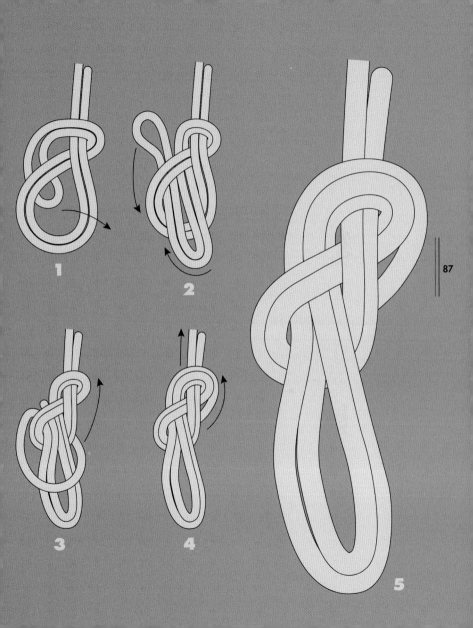

1

2

3

4

5

87

⑤ ◐ ⑤ ◑

Multiloop knots are employed by climbers—in ways that they never were by seamen—because of their need to anchor or belay (perhaps to several fixed points), as well as to improvise chest and seat harnesses. The figure-eight layout is said to be preferable because it is easy to learn and less likely to be tied wrongly by someone who is wet, cold, almost exhausted, and perhaps temporarily unnerved.

In a long bight, form a figure eight (1), but then pull a doubled bight through to create twin loops (2). Bring the tail end of the initial bight around the front of the knot and tuck it down beside the two loops just made to form a third one (3, 4). If tied with a bight made in the end of the rope and not in the middle, back up the end by tying it to the standing part of the rope.

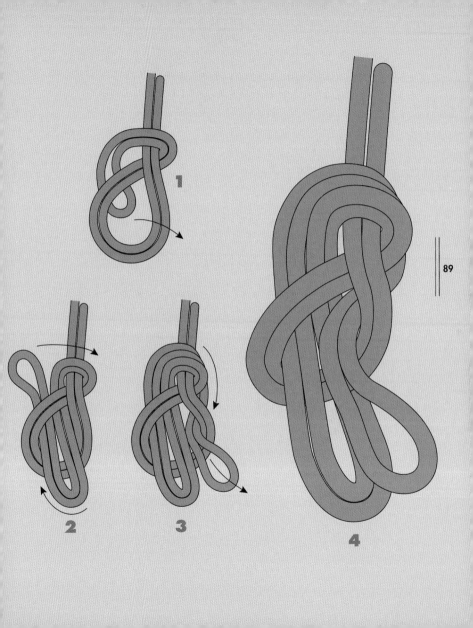

1

2

3

4

89

Butterfly loop   ❺ ❺ ❸ ❺

This knot, also known as the alpine butterfly, is used to put a loop in a section of rope where there will be tension along both standing ends. The butterfly does not greatly weaken the strength of the rope, and is often used by mountaineers to attach a team of climbers along a rope, for protection against a fall.

Start by taking a bight of rope and twisting it into a loop (1). Continue twisting in the same direction to make a second loop above the first (2). Bring the top loop down below the twists (3). Then feed the top of the bight up through the first small loop (4). Pull the slack out of the knot, then pull on the standing ends to tighten (5).

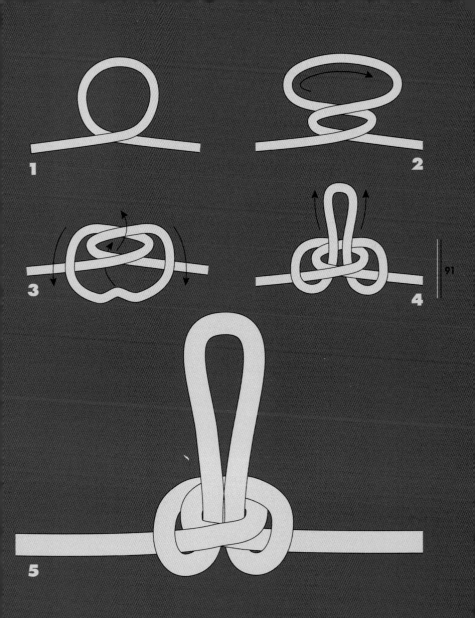

92

Climbers may use this cordage arrangement as an emergency harness of last resort. The discomfort inherent in hanging by it could be somewhat reduced by pulling one of the waist wraps down to form a primitive seat; but anyone suspended by it for too long runs the risk of being dangerously squeezed.

Wrap the rope four times around the waist (1)—although, on a short rope, two or three turns are sufficient—then tuck a loop from the standing part of the rope up beneath these turns (2). Pass the working end down, around the standing part, and back up to tuck through the top of the loop (3). Tighten the knot (4) and then secure the end by tying it around some or all of the waist turns.

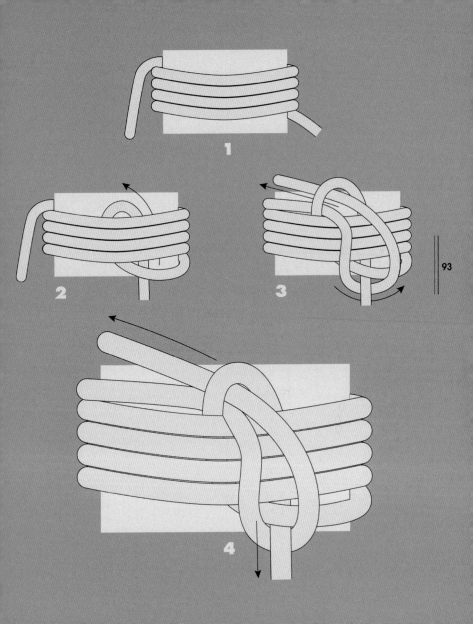

Triple crown loop || ❸ ❸ ❹ ❹

These twin splayed loops are distinctly more fun to tie than the Spanish bowline (*see pages 78–79*) and more good-looking. This knot too is tied, and untied, in the bight.

Start by locating the middle of the rope or cord, then pull down a long bight to create a Y-shape (1). Bring the twin standing parts around and up to lie across the right-hand arm of the Y (2), which in turn is laid down over the Y's left arm (3). Lastly, tuck the left-hand bight down through the circular space created by the two standing parts (4). Carefully tighten the knot, pulling in turn—a bit at a time—on each of the six strands that emerge from the knot, eliminating unwanted crossovers so that each pair lies neat and parallel (5).

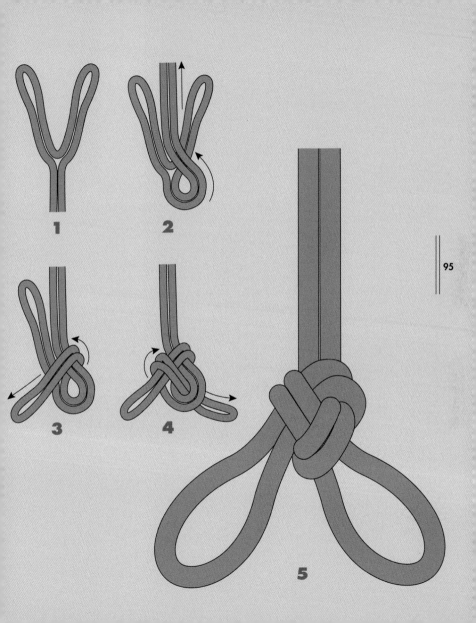

1

2

3

4

5

Frost knot

This webbing knot was devised in the 1960s by Tom Frost for use in making the loops from which the short climbing ladders or stirrups known as étriers (*see page 98*) are suspended. A bulky but strong doubled version is used to tie together separate lengths of webbing for climbers' chest and seat harnesses.

To create an endless strop or sling with a Frost knot, first form a bight in one end; then merely slip the other end into it (1), and tie all three parts in an overhand knot (2). For a bend or joining knot, make a bight in one end of one piece of webbing and tie it in an overhand knot (3); make a similar bight in one end of the other length and follow the first knot around (entering at the bight and leaving at the standing part) (4). Pull it all tight (5).

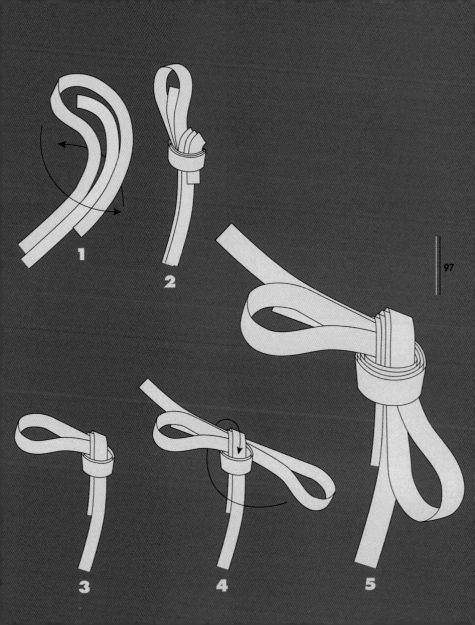

Etrier 5 5 4 2

This is a French word meaning "stirrup," but in climbing and caving it refers to a short stepladder; it may also be called an "aider." Formerly of rope, étriers are now usually made from 1-inch (2.5-cm) webbing, and vary in length from two to five 1-ft (30-cm) foot-loops. Etriers may be factory-made with sewn steps, but can easily be knotted.

Take about 15 ft (4.5 m) of flat, rather than tubular, webbing for a four-step version. Starting with a Frost knot (see pages 96–97), turn the webbing into an endless band, leaving a small loop at the top for the attachment of a carabiner (1). Then tie a series of three overhand knots (see page 292) in both legs of this webbing strop or sling (2, 3), in such a way that one leg of each loop created is shorter than the other (4).

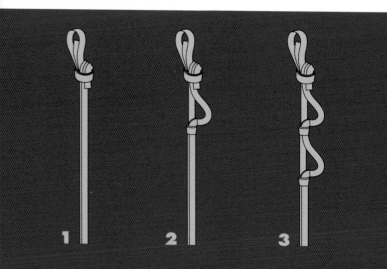

1 **2** **3** **4**

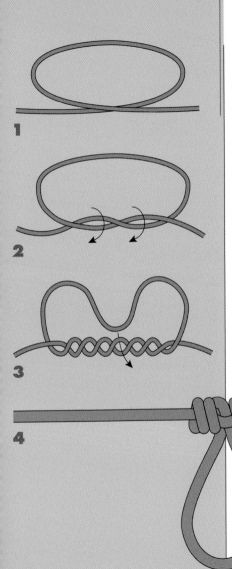

Dropper loop

❹ ❹ ❹ ❶

This knot is used when a string loop is needed in a section of standing line, where the load is distributed along the line rather than directly to the loop. It can be used to rig many hooks and weights from a single fishing line. You must have access to one end of the line to tie this knot, so it cannot be tied between two anchored lines.

Begin by creating a large loop in the line (1). Repeatedly wrap the free end through the loop (2). When you have close to eight wraps, spread open the wrap closest to the middle, creating an "eye" (3). Feed the center of the top of the loop through the eye, moisten, and pull the standing ends to tighten (4).

Lariat knot

3 3 3 3

A horseman's lariat is made by running the standing part of a line through a small fixed loop. The version shown here uses the bowstring loop—the procedure for early American and Spanish horsemen.

Begin with a loop in the standing end, with the working end emerging on top of the loop (1). Pull the working end through the loop from the bottom (2). Feed the working end beneath the adjacent section of knot and it will emerge on the opposite side (3).

Then "flip" the knot so that the loop runs over the standing part of the line (4). The adjustment of the knot makes it possible to make the lariat more or less responsive to inertial forces so that it does not collapse on its way to the steer to be roped.

1

2

3

4

Neck halter

🢂 🢃 🢄 🢅

This fixed loop is a quick and simple contrivance to hold a large but docile domestic animal, or to improvise a neck lanyard for whistle, knife, or stopwatch.

Tie a simple overhand knot at a distance from the end of the rope at least twice the length of the required loop (1). Add a second overhand knot close to the rope's end (2). Tuck the knotted end through the first knot (3) and pull on either side to tighten it (4).

Tucked double overhand loop

This is a robust sliding noose knot with a wide variety of uses in the home and garden, at work and at leisure.

First make a bight. Then take the working end down, around to the back, and up (1). Make a second wrapping turn, to the right of the first, enclosing both legs of the bight (2). Tuck the end through the resulting couple of turns to lie alongside its standing part (3). Pull both the end and the related loop leg apart to tighten the knot (4, 5).

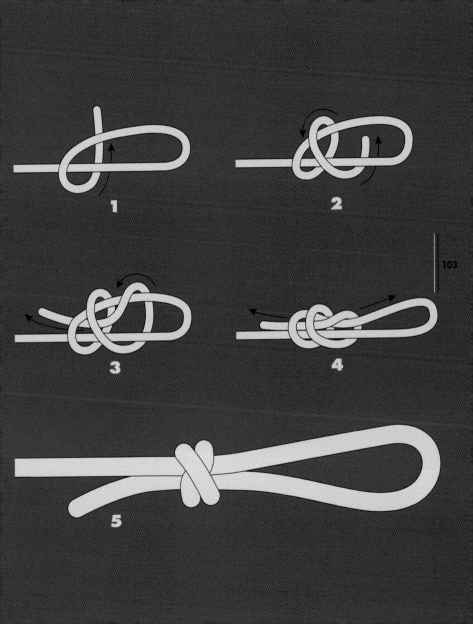

Noose ❷ ❷ ❺ ❺

A noose is any loop that slides along the standing part, but holds firmly round it. This simple noose is a useful way to attach a small line. It can be tied extremely quickly with practice, but is secure enough for light loads.

Start with a loop, with the working end emerging from the bottom (1).

Pull a bight from the standing part through the loop (2).

Pull on the standing part of the bight to create the size of loop desired (3).

Pull the loop further to tighten (4).

104

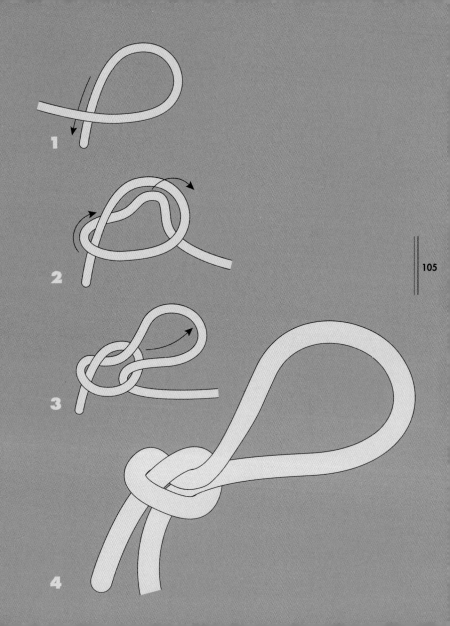

❸ ❹ ❹ ❹

The Englishman's loop is an easily adjustable one. The sliding loop is fixed by adding the last overhand, against which any load will pull, further tightening the knot.

Start with a loop (1). Pull a bight from the working end through the loop, making the bight the same size as the loop you need (2). With the remaining working end, make a loop around the standing part. Feed the working end through the last loop (3, 4), and tighten it by pulling it away from the large loop (5). Pull the large loop to slide the last overhand up snug to the knot, holding the loop in place (6).

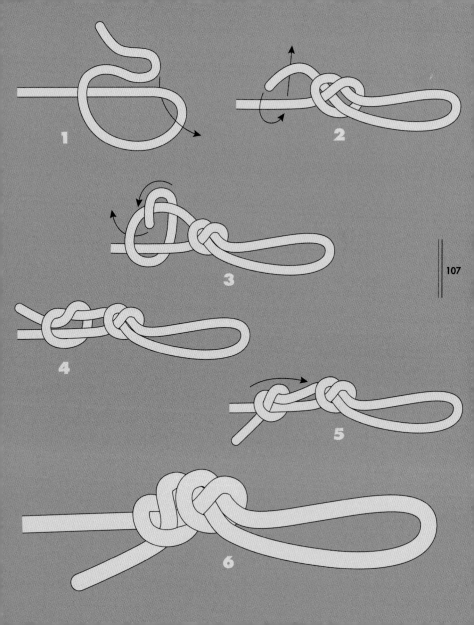

This is another of those knots intended to be tied in the bight. It has been used to secure the middle one of a trio of climbers, but acquired its name from its earlier use in manhandling field guns, when a series of shoulder loops were created in draglines for men to haul upon. In this way it could also ease the load upon horses struggling to pull coaches and carriages uphill, hence its other name of "manharness" knot or hitch. Another application, by horse riders in the US, has been as a static picket-line knot to tether their steeds at overnight campsites.

Make a loop with the working end on top (1). Then pass it beneath the loop just formed (2). Pull the right-hand section of line under, then over, and up through the original loop (3), to replace it and create the final loop (4). Remove any slack by pulling first on both standing parts of the line, and then by tugging on the loop itself (5).

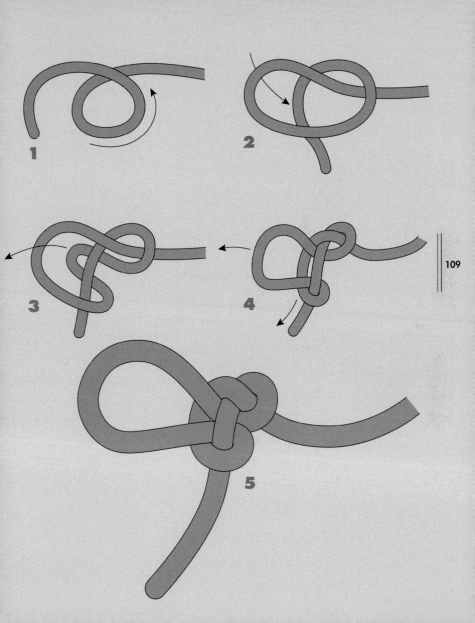

❹ ❺ ❸ ❷

The angler's loop, also called a perfection loop, is most often used as a terminal end to the casting line of fly-fishermen. This casting line is connected to a monofilament leader with a perfection loop on the end as well. They are then locked together by threading one through the other.

Begin with a loop with the working end emerging from the bottom of the loop (1). With the working end, wrap the loop from the top to the bottom, then bring the working end to the top and lay it across the main loop (2). Pull the first wrap up through the loop (3), pulling on all the emerging ends to tighten (4). Trim the excess working end as necessary (5).

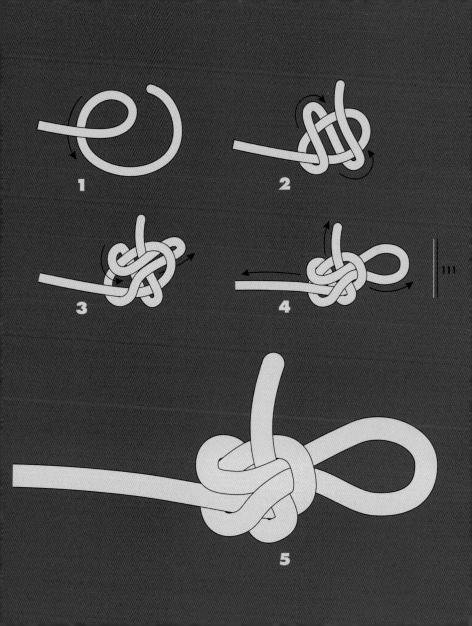

Farmer's loop

This is a knot with an agricultural pedigree—at home on the farm, but handy whenever a fixed loop is needed that must be tied in the bight.

With the working part of the rope, go twice around a wrist or arm, to create two full round turns (1). Now lift up the center wrapping turn and replace it on the right (2). Next, leapfrog the newly created center turn to the left (3), then shift the resulting center knot partway to the right (4). Finally, pull up what has now become the center turn into the required loop (5), remove the knot from the wrist or arm, and tighten the knot (6).

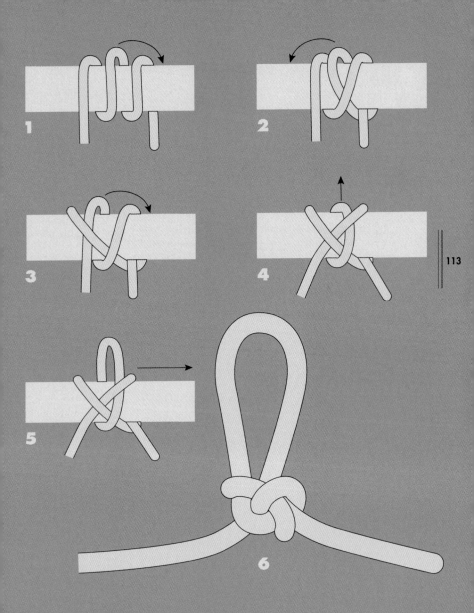

113

Scaffold knot ❺ ❺ ❸ ❷

The scaffold knot forms a string sliding loop that can be placed round a metal eye or some other fixed point. It is a triple overhand noose.

Start with a large loop going through the eye (1). Bring the working end round the whole loop several times (2), working towards the eye. Then feed it through the wraps alongside the standing part (3). Pull the standing line and the working end to tighten (4). Snug the knot up against the eye to finish (5).

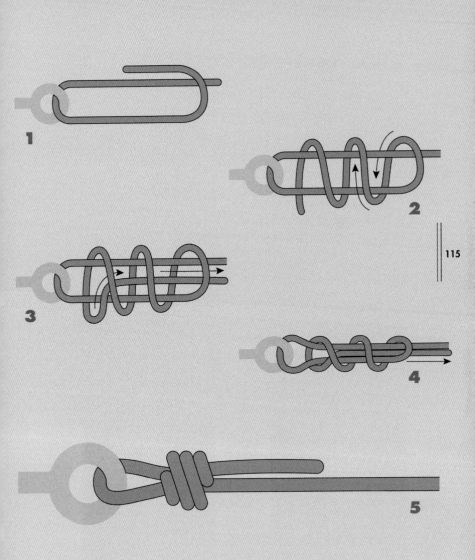

Midshipman's loop

This useful loop is another shock-absorbing, slide-and-grip knot (*see also the adjustable bend, page 29*). Grasp the knot in one hand and you can shift it along the standing part of the rope around which it is tied. Apply a load, however, and it will hold fast—unless overloaded, when it will slide. This characteristic knot can be used to tighten or slacken tent guy-lines and as a third hand in many home repairs. It is not to be confused with the crane-hook hitch of the same name, which was once employed by dock workers handling cargoes between ships and warehouses.

Pass the working end around or through the fixture or load, and cross it in front of the standing part of the line (1). Tuck the end once to encircle the standing part (2), then again above the first turn (3). Take a final turn around the standing part beyond the original crossing point (4). Work the knot snug and tight, since it depends for its friction on creating a dogleg formation in the standing part of the line (5).

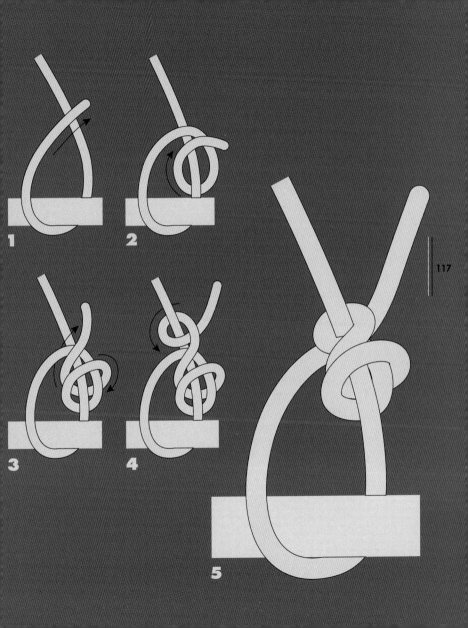

117

True lover's loop

3 5 3 3

Just one of several knots with this name, this consists of twin interlocked overhand or thumb knots, to make a loop in a lanyard or a necklace, from which anything from a lucky mascot to car keys may be suspended.

Locate the middle of the cord and, some distance from the end of the bight, equal to the length of the required loop, tie an overhand knot (1). Pass the other end through this knot, from front to back (2), then tie an identical overhand knot (3); the twin parts in both knots should spiral to the left or counterclockwise. Pull on the left-hand loop and on both ends to tighten the knot (4).

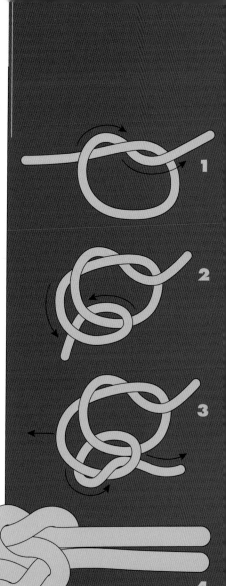

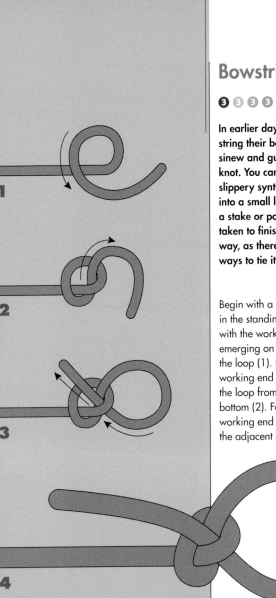

Bowstring loop

❸ ❷ ❸ ❸

In earlier days archers would string their bows with natural sinew and gut by tying this knot. You can still use it to tie slippery synthetic materials into a small loop to attach to a stake or post. Care must be taken to finish it in the right way, as there are several ways to tie it incorrectly.

Begin with a loop in the standing end, with the working end emerging on top of the loop (1). Pull the working end through the loop from the bottom (2). Feed the working end beneath the adjacent section of knot and it will emerge on the opposite side (3). Pull on the standing end to tighten the knot (4). In slippery materials, the knot can be made tighter even when under a load, but will not loosen.

Trident loop ❸ ⑤ ❷ ❸

Robert M. Wolfe, MD, of Chicago, Illinois, devised this knot for climbers as an alternative to the figure-eight loop, and began to promote it in 1995. The greater tensile strength of the latest climbing ropes compensates for the fact that the trident loop is somewhat weaker than the one it is intended to replace; however, it is remarkably secure (in shock-loading tests it yielded not a millimeter). Take care that each stage is done correctly: one mistaken tuck or turn will result in something less reliable.

Tie an overhand knot, far enough away from the working end to allow for the size of loop intended (1). Bring the end around to form the loop (2), then lay a small bight over the belly of the initial overhand knot and tuck it through between the two entwined knot parts (3). Tighten the knot a bit at a time until all of the slack has been eliminated. Finally, pass the working end around and in front of the standing part of the line, before tucking it to tie a retaining half hitch (4, 5).

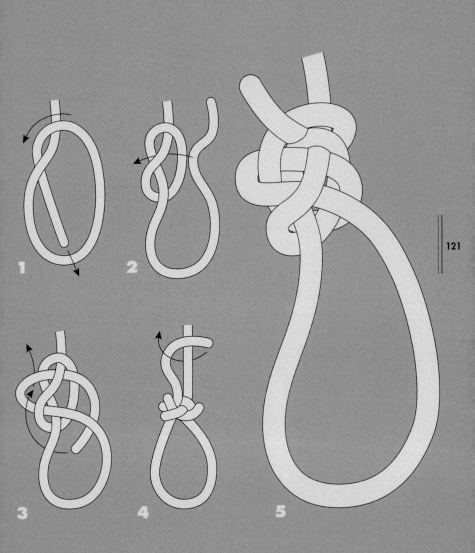

1

2

3

4

5

121

Bimini twist

5 4 3 1

This long loop is the start for any deepwater big game-fishing tackle system. Knots generally weaken, to some degree or other, the lines in which they are tied; but lines in which this knot is tied remain—it is claimed—as strong as if they had never been knotted. Tying this paragon, however, requires coordination.

Make a bight at least 3 ft (1 m) long, which must then be twisted 20 or more times (1). This can be crudely done by inserting a finger and forcing the bight around as if tightening a tourniquet; but is more expertly achieved with two hands by twiddling each leg of the bight in opposite directions. Either way, both feet must then be inserted into the remaining loop and spread sideways, with one hand at the same time bracing the standing end of the line vertical, while the other holds the tag end out sideways (2). These actions create a layer of wrapping turns that—when fed and controlled by the hand holding the tag end—run down and cover the initial twists, some of which are sacrificed to permit this development (3). Add at least three extra wrapping turns to trap the tag end (4, 5). The result is a slender, tubelike loop knot (6).

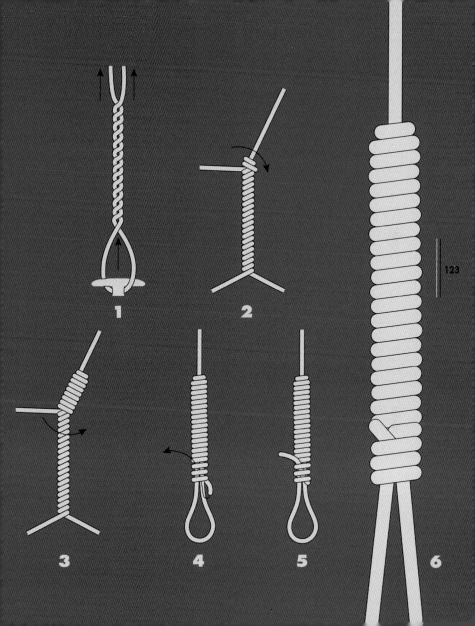

1 2 3 4 5 6

123

Hitches

Hitches form a large family of knots and generally attach a rope to a ring, rail, or post, although occasionally they may also join one rope to another rope, or even to itself. Hitches that incorporate a drawloop (such as the slipped cleat hitch) provide a quick release when only a temporary hold is required. The half hitch and clove hitch play a role in many different knots.

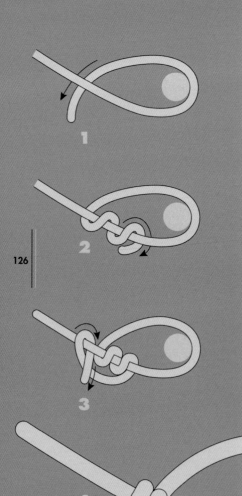

Taut-line hitch

❸ ❸ ❸ ❹

As its name implies, this hitch is used to put tension on a standing line, making it taut. It is most useful for temporary guy-lines attached to a post in the ground. It can be used for tightening clothes-lines and the like, but will release under heavy loads.

Begin by passing the line around the post and crossing it under the loaded line (1). Wrap it around the loaded line once on the side of the crossing closest to the post, then wrap it around again (2). Bring the remaining line out to the side away from the post and cross it over the weighted line. Wrap it around the weighted line, and tuck it under itself to finish the knot (3). Tighten the taut line hitch by pulling the lines emerging from the sides of the knot away and slightly toward the middle of the knot (4).

Lobster-buoy hitch ❸ ❹ ❹ ❹

Knots rely, one way or another, on friction for their holding power. Quick and simple knots can, therefore, be less effective. But the lobster-buoy hitch (like the buntline hitch, *see pages 212–213*) traps its end inside the knot, pressing it against the anchorage point, and in this way gains added security.

Make a turn around rail, ring, or spar, then lead the working end behind the standing part of the line below the initial turn, and tuck it through the loop that has been formed (1). Go around the standing part once more (2), and tuck the end back beneath itself (3). Slide the knot up to the anchorage point (4).

1

2

3

4

A trucker's hitch—in earlier times known as a wagoner's hitch—is the general name for several pulley-like cordage contrivances that secure the load on any kind of cart, carriage, or motor vehicle by tightening its lashing around a convenient anchor point. Some are speedily applied and untied again, but can spill if not carefully done; others, of which this is an example, take a few more seconds to tie (and untie) but are more reliable.

Bring the end of the line or lashing close to its anchorage and tie a tucked figure-eight knot (1, 2). Lead the working end around the anchorage (3) and through the figure-eight bight (4). Pull down on the end to impart tension, then tie the working end off with two half hitches (see page 130) (5, 6, 7).

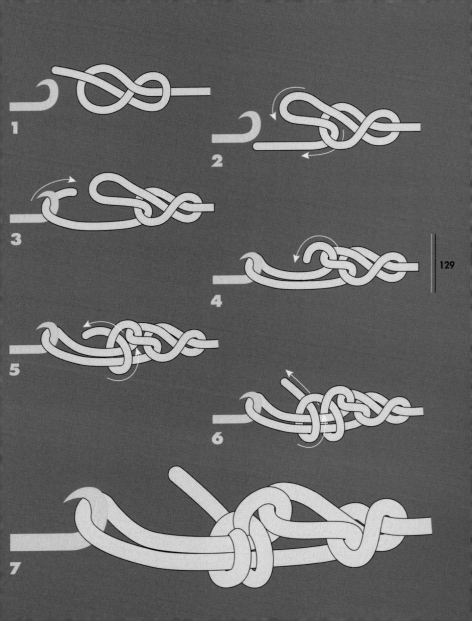

Half hitch

⬤ ⬤ ⬤ ⬤

The half hitch is a very simple but insecure hitch. It can be used temporarily for light loads, but should never be relied on for heavy or safety loads.

Begin by passing the rope around the spar or post to which you are hitching it (1). Then pass the working end around the loaded end, and feed it between the post and the loop to form the hitch (2). Pull the loaded end to tighten the knot (3).

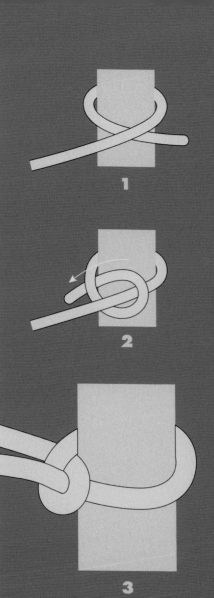

Slippery half hitch

When a very fast, quick-release hitch is needed, a slippery half hitch is often used. Although it is not a strong knot, it is easy to tie and untie, making it a favorite for quick jobs around the house and store.

First run the working end through or around the object (1). Then bring the working end behind the standing part (2) and pull a bight through the loop from the front (3). Pull on the bight and the standing end to tighten the knot (4). A quick pull on the free end of the bight will release it.

131

Two half hitches ❷ ❸ ❹ ❹

For greater strength and resistance to slipping than is offered by the half hitch, use two half hitches rather than one.

Start by passing the rope around the post to which you are hitching it (1). Then pass the working end around the loaded end, and feed it between the post and the loop to form the hitch (2). Repeat the process by passing the working end around the loaded end again and feeding it through to make a second half hitch (3). Pull the loaded end to tighten the knot (4). The hitches should slide to tighten around the post.

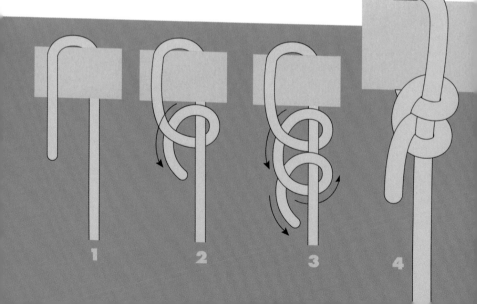

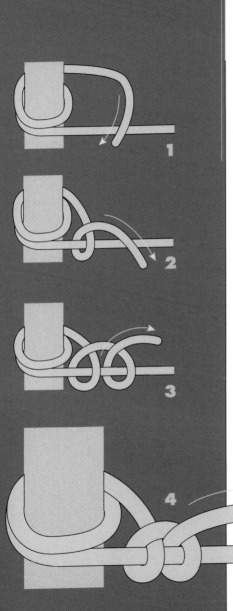

Round turn and two half hitches

4 5 4 4

This knot offers an effective way to attach to a post or spar a line that will be made taut and does not need to be adjusted. Security and strength are provided by adding the round turns: these take most of the weight of the load, while the hitches keep it in place.

Start by wrapping the rope around the post or spar for two complete turns (1). Pass the working end over and around the standing part, then feed it between the post and the standing part (2).

Bring the working end away from the post and make another wrap around the standing part, again feeding the working end between the previous wrap and the standing part (3). Pull on the working end and cinch the knot up to the post to tighten (4).

Sliding sheet bend hitch

This is yet another slide-and-grip knot. The drawloop enables it to be readily undone again. Use it for jobs as diverse as temporarily mooring a small boat or tethering a grazing animal.

Lead the working end of the line around one side of the anchorage point, and at the same time pull a bight along the other side (1). Tie a half hitch around this bight (2), then make a locking tuck by pulling a final bight from the working end through beside the half hitch (3, 4). Take care in tightening the knot (5, 6) to avoid distorting and capsizing it.

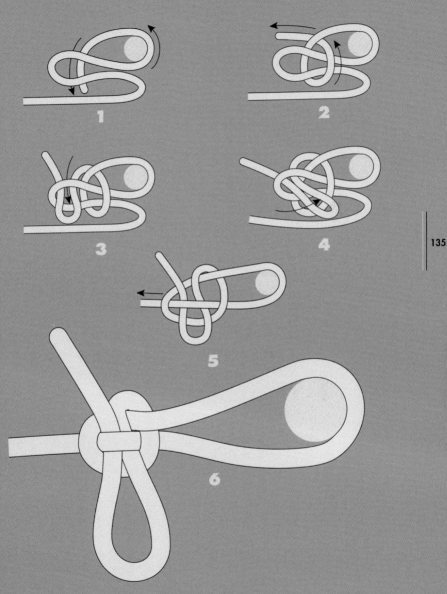

Cow hitch ❸ ❷ ❺ ❺

A quick and easy way to attach any sort of cordage to a post or rail, this is a very insecure hitch, unsuitable for heavy work (let alone tethering a cow), because the load falls upon only one leg of the doubled bight with which it is formed.

Double the working end of the line to create a bight (1), and pass it around the intended anchorage point (2). Then simply pull both long and short ends through the bight (3) and tighten the knot (4).

Slipped noose hitch ❸ ❸ ❹ ❺

This temporary attachment has a drawloop to enable quick release from the hitch.

Drape the rope or cord over the hitching rail, then take the working end around the standing part and back to the front once more (1). Tie an overhand knot (2), but leave a drawloop protruding and do not pull the end completely through the knot (3). Pull on the loop and the standing end to tighten (4).

Knute hitch

❹ ⓸ ⓹ ⓹

US master rigger, writer, and broadcaster Brion Toss seems to have come up with the name, in 1990, for this simplest of knots, which is probably centuries old. Use it to attach a lanyard to a tool, to bend a halyard to a sail, or for any other purpose that can be imagined.

Simply tuck a bight through a tight hole and add an overhand knot (*see page 292*) as a stopper (1). Then tuck the knotted end of the lanyard or cord through the bight (2) and pull the arrangement tight (3).

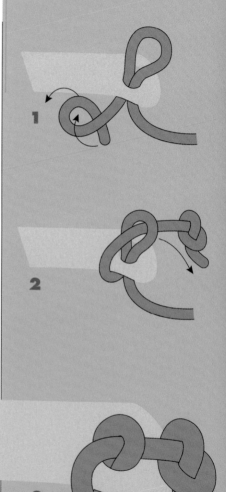

Girth hitch

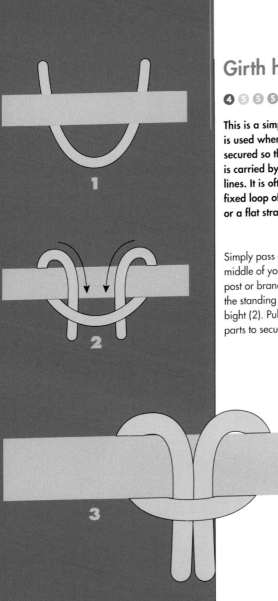

④ ⑤ ⑤ ⑤

This is a simple knot, which is used when a line must be secured so that equal weight is carried by both emerging lines. It is often tied using a fixed loop of rope, webbing, or a flat strap.

Simply pass a bight from the middle of your line behind a post or branch (1). Then feed the standing parts through the bight (2). Pull on the standing parts to secure the knot (3).

Munter friction hitch

Since this climber's knot was first introduced in 1974 at a meeting of the Union Internationale des Associations d'Alpinisme, in Italy, it is also sometimes referred to as the Italian hitch. In kernmantel (core-and-sheath) rope it is widely used to absorb energy through friction, whether it is being used for lowering a load under control or checking an unwanted fall.

Start by forming an uncompleted overhand knot (1), then enclose the two knot parts as illustrated within a gated carabiner (2). If the strain is relaxed from one part of the rope and imposed on the other—for example, taking in slack, as opposed to gradually letting it out—it is acceptable for the knot to slip around into a reverse layout (3).

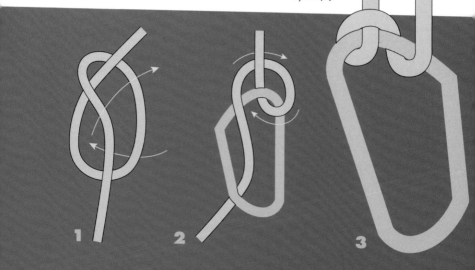

1

2

3

Munter mule

⁂ ④ ④ ④ ④

Each and every knot may be tied left-handed or right-handed, having a distinct mirror image, and—to illustrate this—the other Munter friction hitch is shown here. To tie off either version (while it is loaded) and then to release it again, for instance to free a hand for some essential extra task, use the Munter mule.

After tying the Munter friction hitch (*see page 140*), pick up a bight in the rope, pass it around the loaded standing part, and tuck it down through its own loop (1) to tie an overhand knot. Secure the end with another overhand knot (2).

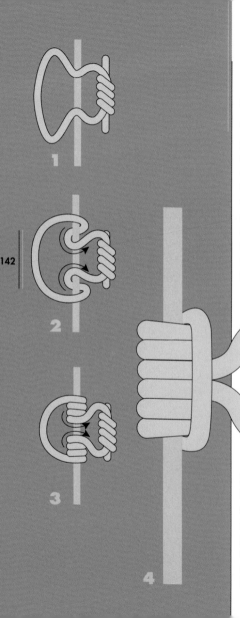

Prusik knot

4 4 4 5

The Prusik (named after an Austrian professor of music) is used to hitch a small loop of rope to a larger one, so that the hitch can be slid up and down the line and locked when loaded. It is used in caving, rescue, and climbing. It does not damage the ropes, as a mechanical ascending device would; it does slip, however, if the diameters of the ropes are not well matched.

Begin with a closed loop of accessory cord (*see the double fisherman's bend on page 19*) (1). Make a wrap around the main line with the loop and pass the knotted end through the loop (2). Continue passing the knotted end around the main line and through the loop again (3). Pull the knotted end to tighten (4). Be very careful to contour the knot correctly as shown, to enable it to work properly. And ensure that the double fisherman's knot in the loop is to one side, rather than directly in the path of the load, when the Prusik is in use.

142

Anchor hitch

This knot is useful to bend a fixed line to a ring or anchor. It does not loosen under moderate motion—something that is required of a hitch for boat anchorage.

Small craft still attach anchors by means of rope rather than chain, and the anchor hitch is a fine choice for such a purpose.

Start by making two turns around the ring from back to front (1). Pass the working end behind the standing part, then through the round turns, from left to right (2). Bring the working end behind the standing part, then wrap upward one turn, feeding the end behind the working part, thus creating a half hitch (3). Pull on the standing part to tighten the knot (4).

143

1   **2**   **3**   **4**

Penberthy knot ❺ ❺ ❹ ❺

Devised by Larry Penberthy and Dick Mitchell in about 1969, this is also known as the caver's helical knot. It is one of a number of sliding friction knots that evolved prior to the advent of mechanical devices, and has the advantage that—unlike some others—it is not prone to jamming.

Take a length of accessory cord and wrap a number of spiral turns around the main climbing rope (1, 2). How many turns will depend on the user's weight: too few and it will slip, but too many will make it difficult to shift. Secure them with a bowline (*see page 63*) (3, 4, 5), adjusting the knot to tighten the spiral turns around the rope (6). As with the turns, and depending again on the load, too much or too little slack within those turns will render the knot hard to move or will allow it to slip.

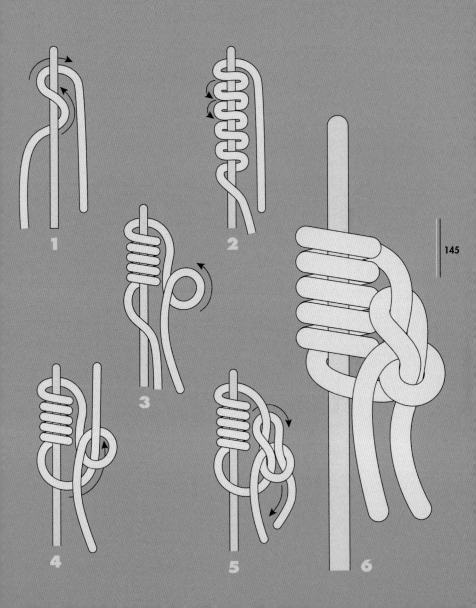

146

This is another of those slide-and-grip, or friction, knots tied by climbers and cavers in accessory cord around climbing ropes. It is used to provide additional security in the activity known as prusiking.

Wrap the accessory cord once around the rope (1). Make a total of four wrapping turns (2), then bring the working end down, over its own standing part, and behind the rope (3). Tuck it up through two of the wrapping turns (4). Where the end emerges, add a figure-eight stopper knot (5).

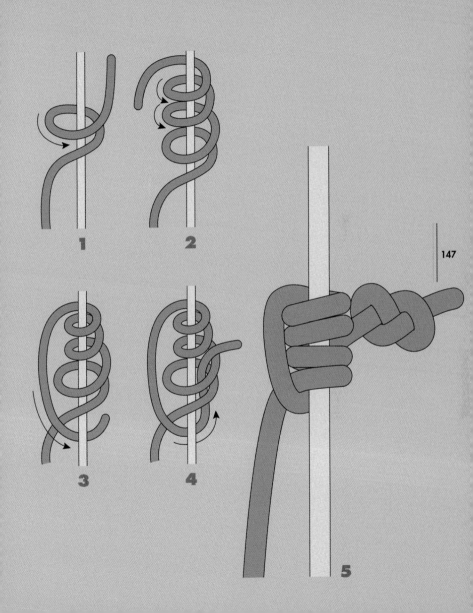

1

2

3

4

5

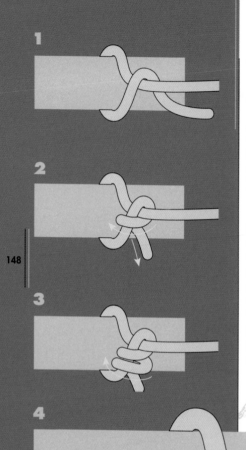

Timber hitch

❷ ❸ ❹ ❹

A timber hitch was traditionally used to drag or hoist a log or pole. The knot will cinch tight against the log when a pull is applied.

Begin the knot by making a turn around the log, then wrap the working end once around the standing end (1). Make a wrap between the working end and the log (2). Then make a second wrap in the same way (3). Pull on the standing end to tighten the knot (4).

Killick hitch

4 4 4 4

When a timber hitch is
followed by several half
hitches along the length of
the pole, it becomes a killick
hitch. This knot distributes
the pull along the length
of the log and keeps it
oriented in one direction.
It is a good improvement
on the timber hitch.

149

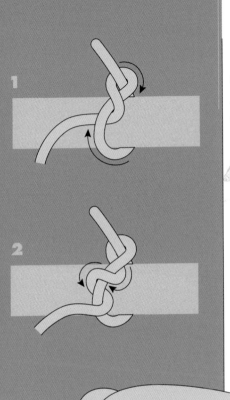

Begin the knot
by making a turn
around the log. Then
wrap the working
end once around the
standing end, and
make several wraps
between the working
end and the log (1,
2). Make a loop in
the free section of the
standing part. Invert
the loop
and place it
over the end
of the log,
opposite the timber
hitch (3). Maneuver
the loop down to
about 1 ft (30 cm)
from the timber hitch.
Repeat this process
until you reach the
end of the log.

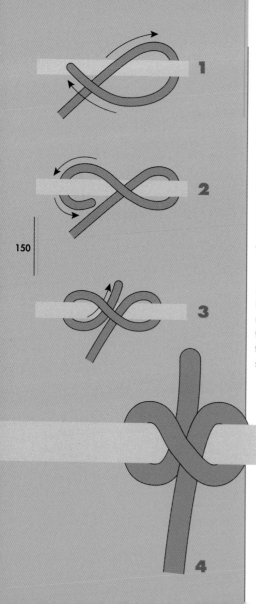

Clove hitch

● ● ● ●

This knot offers a fast, easy way to secure a line to a post or spar. It is often used in climbing as a temporary tie-in to an anchor point. The clove hitch will not bind after a load, and is therefore easy to untie; only under a very high load will this hitch fail, although it can be insecure.

Start by passing the line around the post (1). Pass it around the post a second time, going in the same direction, but making sure that the second wrap goes across the loaded line from the first wrap (2). Feed the free end underneath the second wrap, keeping it next to the post (3). Make sure there are at least a few inches of line left past the hitch away from the loaded end. Cinch the whole knot tight to complete the knot (4).

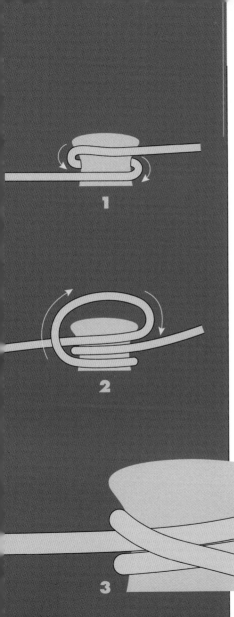

Clove hitch II

❸ ❸ ❺ ❺

The clove hitch (*see page 150*) is commonly used to suspend from, or attach to, a horizontal metal rail or wooden spar items as varied as a boat's fender or some working part of a weaving loom. But it can also be used to brake or check the run of anything—boat, horse, or loaded wheelbarrow—that might otherwise go out of control.

To utilize the knot in this dynamic way, first cast an underhand loop (that is, one in which the end lies beneath the loaded part of the line) around a belaying post or other fixed anchorage point (1).

The friction this creates will render the weight manageable. Once no further movement is necessary, add a second underhand loop to complete the knot (2, 3). Caution: the clove hitch is a temporary hitch, so if the knot is likely to remain in place for a long time, exchange it for one of the more secure hitches illustrated elsewhere in this section.

Strangle knot

5 5 4 2

One of a number of binding knots, originally used by millers and in granaries to tie up the necks of flour and grain sacks, this is perhaps the neatest and most secure of the bunch. Its earliest publication seems to have been in the 1916 Swedish knot book *Om Knutar* ("On Knots") by Hjalmar Öhrvall; but up-to-date applications include anything where a quick and temporary seizing is required, from whipping a cut rope's end to attaching a pencil to a clipboard.

Tie an overhand knot and tuck the working end a second time (1). Pull steadily on both ends, allowing them to twist in opposite directions, so that the loop wraps and spirals around the entwined knot parts (2). Pull both ends to tighten the knot, and jam it around whatever is to be bound (3).

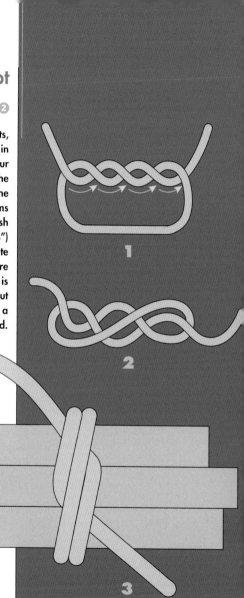

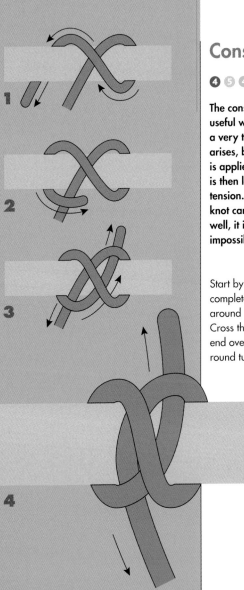

Constrictor knot

④ ⑤ ④ ①

The constrictor is extremely useful when the need for a very tight binding knot arises, because any pull that is applied to the free ends is then locked under its own tension. But because this knot can be tightened so well, it is often nearly impossible to untie.

Start by making a complete round turn around the object. Cross the working end over in a second round turn, on the opposite side from the first (1). Bring the working end to the front of the knot (2). Feed the working end beneath both loops between the object and the line (3). By pulling the two ends, this knot will become very tight, binding the object (4).

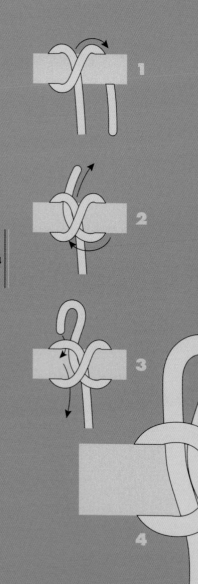

Slipped constrictor knot

❺ ④ ④ ❺

The basic constrictor knot is a semi-permanent binding which, when tightened, can often be removed only by cutting it off. Incorporating a drawloop provides a quick release for applications where only a temporary seizing is required.

First, create a constrictor knot: make a complete round turn around the object, then cross the working end over in a second round turn, on the opposite side from the first (1). Bring the working end to the front of the knot and feed it beneath both loops between the object and the line (2). Then bend the end back in a bight (3) and retrace its initial pathway, going under two knot parts. Tighten the knot by pulling on both standing parts, but not the working end (4).

Poldo tackle

This ingenious tensioning device has been around in one form or another since at least the eighteenth century; and is named after Poldo Izzo, an Italian sailing instructor. It can be applied to a clothesline, a tent guy-line, or in any other situation where a taut line must periodically be slackened off, then tightened again.

Tie an angler's loop (*see pages 110–111*) in one end of a line, which must be at least three times the length of the required range of movement in the completed tackle (1). Pass the other end through the knotted eye, leaving a large running loop (2), then make a second loop by passing the working end through the first loop (3). Tie another angler's loop (4). To apply tension, pull the two knots apart; to release it, push them together.

155

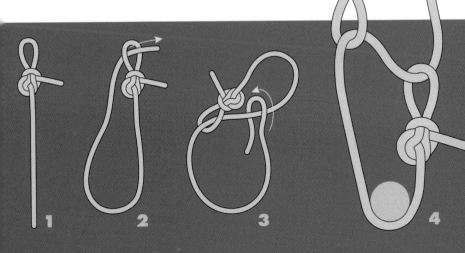

1 **2** **3** **4**

Boa knot ❺⑤❸❸

This beefed-up binding is associated with the British weaver Peter Collingwood, who first publicized it for himself in 1996, although others later claimed to have known and used the knot at least 10 years earlier. He employed it to bind the ends of braids that had to be cut off close alongside the knot itself. It is, as its name implies, related to the constrictor knot (*see pages 153–154*).

Lay down two matching loops, the second atop the first (1), and spread them into a coil (2). Turn the right-hand half of this coil up and away through 180°, or half a circle (3). Insert through the two halves of the resulting figure-eight layout whatever is to be seized, going under-over-under (4), and then turn the knot over to work it tight (5).

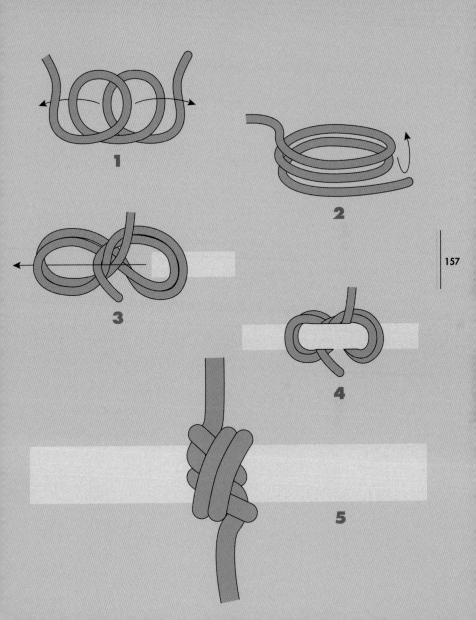

1

2

3

157

4

5

Heddon knot

This knot was invented by Chet Heddon in 1959. It is also called a kreuzklem and may be referred to as a cross-Prusik knot. Tied in accessory cord or (better still) webbing, it is as effective as the classic Prusik knot (*see page 142*), but more easily loosened.

Pass the bight from one end of a sling around the climbing rope (1, 2). Wrap the body of the sling in the opposite direction, to go over the bight (3) and then tuck through it (4). The load must be exerted downward (5).

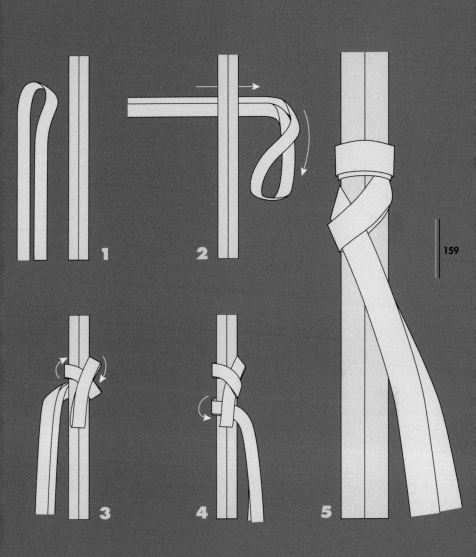

Double Heddon knot

The extra turn of this reinforced Heddon knot (*see pages 158–159*) generates additional friction and load-bearing, while making it harder to loosen. It works best with webbing.

Arrange the bight of a webbing sling around the climbing rope (1), and trap it with two wrapping turns (2, 3). Tuck the other end of the sling through the bight (4) and load downward (5).

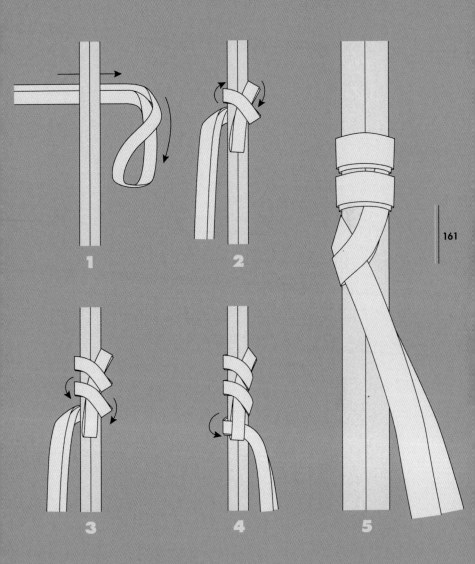

Release hitch

Release hitches are an attempt to avoid the shortcomings of some other prusiking knots. A "load end" wraps around the rappel rope, while a "release end" runs parallel to it and is enclosed by the wrapping turns. Loading causes the turns to tighten and grip, whereas a tug on the release end results in them slipping. These two were devised by Robert Chisnall some 20 years ago. Each has its advantages. The top-loaded version releases easily, but will slide several feet as it tightens under a load if it is slack to start with; conversely, the bottom-loaded knot grips when even sloppily tied, but (when loaded) the release end has to be tugged very hard to cause slippage.

Method 1 (top-loaded): with the load end, wrap upward five or six times, enclosing the release end (1, 2). Tighten this knot methodically, then tighten it again before use (3). Method 2 (bottom-loaded): create the figure-eight layout illustrated and wrap downward with the load end, so that both ends emerge at the bottom of the knot (1, 2). Tighten the knot before use (3).

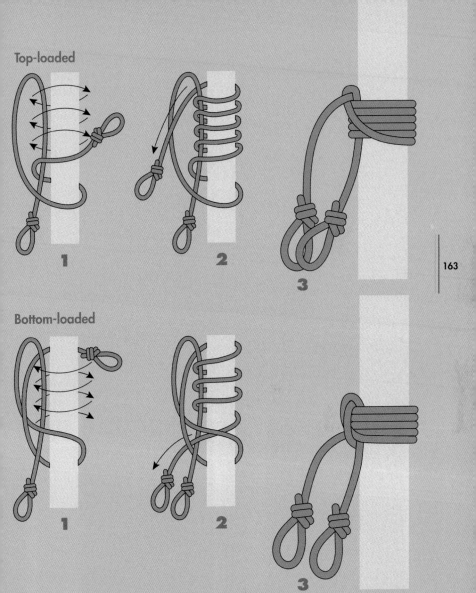

Top-loaded

1

2

3

163

Bottom-loaded

1

2

3

Klemheist knot

This is a prusiking knot (occasionally referred to as the Headon knot) that is designed to cope with a load that pulls directly downward. Do not use it on a traverse rope. It may also be tied in webbing, but may be more efficient in cord.

Wrap a sling or strop three or four times around the main climbing rope (1, 2), then tuck the lower bight through the upper one (3) and pull it down to tighten the arrangement (4, 5). Load it downward; if it tends to slip, add more wrapping turns. When unloaded, it slides upward more easily than the classic Prusik knot (*see page 142*).

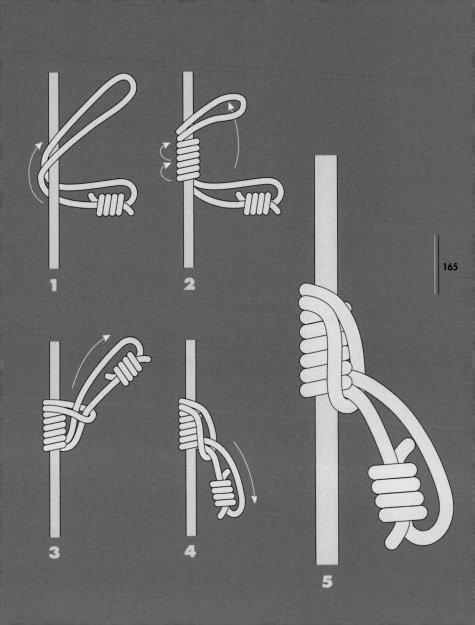

1

2

3

4

5

Bachman knot ❹ ❹ ❹ ❹

This is believed to be the oldest of the semi-mechanical climbing knots and originated in Austria. The knot works well on wet or icy ropes and is easier to slide up the rope than the older Prusik knot, or indeed a Klemheist. Use it on single or double climbing ropes, but only when it is downloaded; do not use this knot on a traverse rope. It is used in self-rescue situations and to hoist a casualty by means of a pulley system.

Clip a sling into a screw-gate carabiner (1), then wind it around the main climbing rope in a descending spiral (2), at the same time enclosing the back bar of the carabiner (3, 4). Load it downward (5).

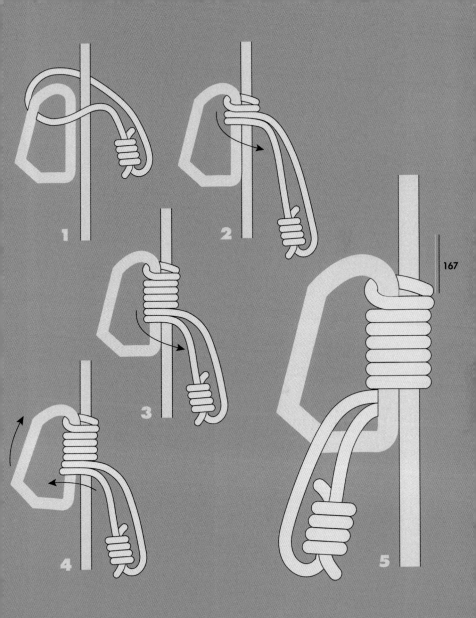

Lighterman's hitch

This hitch has long been used by longshoremen, riggers, and watermen to tie one boat to another or to belay a mooring or a guy-line. Its great advantages are that it is extremely secure, although it will not jam, and that it is easily cast off when necessary.

Make a turn (or several, as required for the job in hand) about the post, rail, or spar so that the strain is taken up (1). Then take a bight beneath the standing part of the line (2) and hitch the bight over the post (3). Wrap the working end around the standing part (4) and then around the post once more (5). Then let it hang (6).

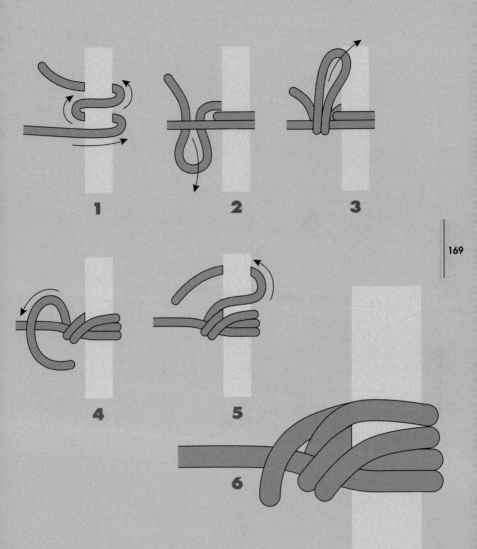

Spar hitch

Besides attaching a rope's end to a horizontal spar, tying this knot in the bight makes it possible to fasten the standing part of a barrier rope or tape to a vertical post, at locations as diverse as country fairs, road construction sites, and crime scenes.

Take the rope around the rail or post, picking up the rear portion and bringing it diagonally across on top of itself (1). Pull out a small bight, twist it counterclockwise, and pass it over the end of the anchorage (2). Then pull on both ends to tighten the knot (3).

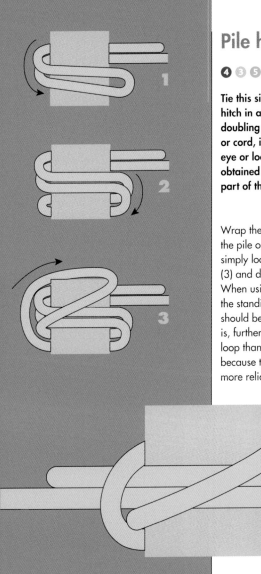

Pile hitch

❹ ❸ ❺ ❺

Tie this simple but effective hitch in a bight made by doubling the end of a rope or cord, in a pre-formed eye or loop, or in a bight obtained from the standing part of the line.

Wrap the bight once around the pile or post (1, 2), then simply loop it over the end (3) and draw it up tight (4). When using a rope's end, the standing part of the line should be underneath (that is, further from the retaining loop than the working end), because that way the knot is more reliable.

The standard cleat hitch is commonly used for the temporary mooring of boats at docks and slips. Cleats are generally positioned regularly around the docking area for convenient tying off. A temporary mooring for a string of boats can be made with the cleat hitch, which is well known among those who enjoy "messing about in boats."

Begin the cleat hitch by passing the line around the entire cleat, beneath the horn away from the boat, then around the horn near the boat. Take the line diagonally across the cleat to the opposite horn (1). Pass the line beneath the horn, then take it diagonally across the cleat again to the horn closest to the boat (2). This time put a loop in the line, and turn it over so that the working end comes from the bottom of the loop (3). Hook the loop over the horn closest to the boat and pull the working end to tighten the hitch (4).

1　**2**　**3**　**4**

Slipped cleat hitch ❸ ② ④ ⑤

A cleat is the piece of hardware with two projecting horns or arms fitted at the foot of flagpoles, sailboat masts, and anywhere else that a halyard or other line is frequently made fast. Knowledgeable riggers attach cleats at an angle of about 10° from the vertical, since this is said to reduce the chances of turns jamming; but a simple quick-release hitch works as well (provided the load keeps a steady pressure on what is a very minimal holdfast).

Make a turn around the bottom of the cleat, then wrap a tight diagonal to the top (1). Bring the rope around the horn (2) and tuck a bight beneath the diagonal just created (3).

1

2

3

Modified clinch knot ❸ ◔ ◔ ❶

This is the preferred knot for attaching artificial lures to monofilament line in most freshwater fishing for medium-sized fish in lakes and rivers. It is used with spin-fishing gear and is easy to tie. It leaves a straight hitch to the eye of the lure to reduce unwanted spinning on the surface and underwater. Like most fishing knots, it is not intended to be untied, because it is far easier to clip the knot off and retie.

Begin by running about 1 ft (30 cm) of line through the eye of the lure (1). Make at least four wraps around the standing line, working away from the eye (2). Bring the working end back through the loop attachment to the eye (3). Then bring the end back down under the last wrap, next to the standing line and the wraps (4). This is what makes this a "modified" clinch. Be sure to moisten the line, and pull both ends to tighten (5). Cinch the wraps closely against the eye to finish (6).

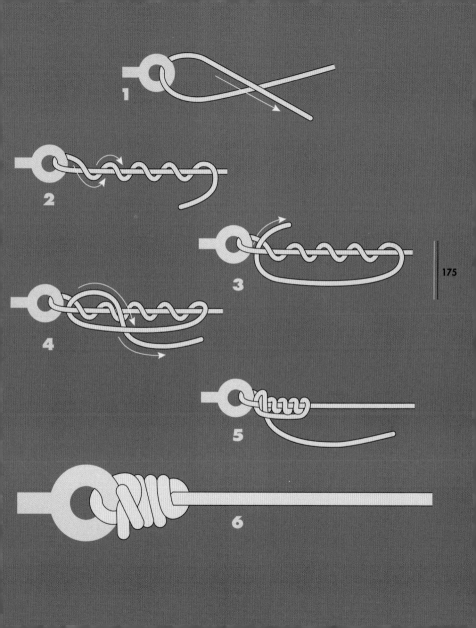

Pedigree cow hitch

This is a more reliable version of the common cow hitch (*see page 136*), as popularized by Harry Asher in his *The Alternative Knot Book* and subsequently adopted by the Girl Guides Association for the first level of its Knotter's Badge. It makes a good multipurpose hitch that is simple to tie.

Pass the working end of the line around the post, spar, or rail (1), then take it across the front of the standing line (2) and up behind the post again (3). Then pass it down through the loop just created (4). Now make the variation that makes this a "pedigree" hitch: tuck and trap the short end of the line through the knot you have just made (5, 6). If you wish, you can leave a drawloop as a means of quick release.

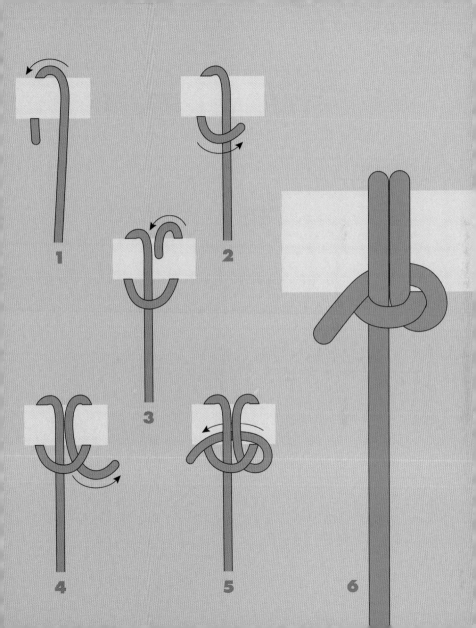

Palomar knot ❸ ◗ ◗ ❸

This fairly strong and very secure knot attaches a fishing line to a hook or lure. Since a bight must be passed over the item of hardware during the tying process, this precludes using the knot on ambitious tackle rigs.

Form a long bight in the end of the line, pass it through the eye (1), then tie an overhand knot (2). Loop the bight over the hook (or bring the hook up through it) (3). Tighten the knot snugly alongside the eye (4).

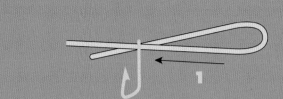

Trilene knot

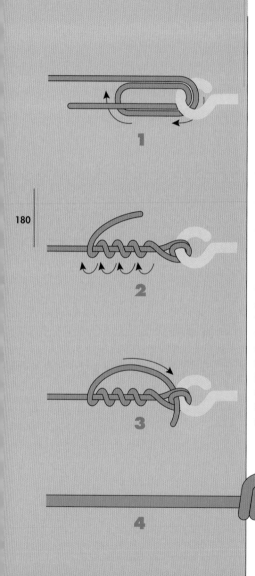

④ ④ ③ ①

The trilene (or Berkley trilene) knot is a fishing knot, used by anglers on swivels and hooks, which has withstood the twentieth-century evolution from horsehair, gut, and silk fishing lines to synthetic monofilaments. It works best in thinner lines, being troublesome to tighten in thicker ones.

Pass the tag end twice through the eye of the hook or swivel to form a round turn (1), then wrap four or five times around the standing part of the line (2). Bring the end forward once more and tuck it down through the round turn originally created (3). Painstakingly pull, push, and knead the knot into its final compact form (4). Familiarity with multifold overhand knots (*see page 300*) will be useful at this stage.

King sling

🏅 🏅 🏅 🏅

Use this angling knot as the basis for a leader system. Its other name is an "end loop knot," and it is suitable for braided lines as well as monofilament. Tying is achieved in seconds.

Make a bight in the end of the line and bend it back on itself (1). Then wrap it at least three times around the doubled standing part (2). Tuck the end of the bight back through the small loop created by the wrapping turns (3), and tighten the knot by pulling the standing part and tag end away from the loop (4).

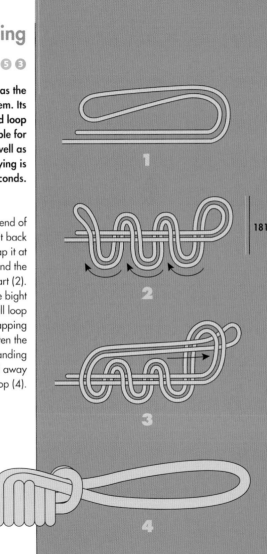

Pitzen knot ④ ③ ② ①

This is another knot to enable anglers to attach a fishing line to a hook, lure, or swivel. It is easy to tie—as fishermen's knots go—and the result is neat and compact.

Put the working end through the eye of the hook or other item, then bring it back to lie alongside its own standing part (1). Make a series of four or five tight wrapping turns, in the direction of the hook, around both sections of the line (2, 3), then bring the end back and tuck it through beneath the first wrapping turn (4). Pull the knot tight with several strong tugs (5). Snip off the tag end close to the knot (6).

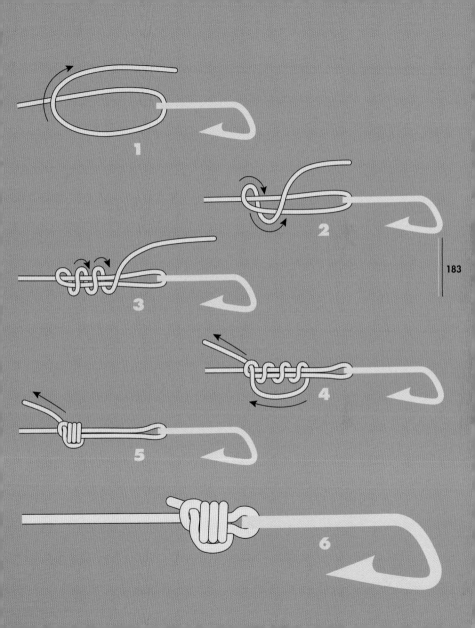

184

This fixed-loop knot is superior to some angling loops in terms of strength and slip resistance.

Tie an overhand knot (*see page 292*) a few inches or centimeters from the end of the line, then pass the line around the eye or ring and back through the knot, re-entering on the same side as it emerged (1). Wrap the line around the standing part (2, 3)—as many as seven times for the thinnest lines, but fewer in stronger lines, and as few as three in the thickest ones. Finally, tuck the tag end back through the knot alongside the standing part (4). Tighten the wrapping turns and then the entire knot, before trimming the end off close to it (5).

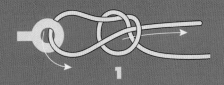

1

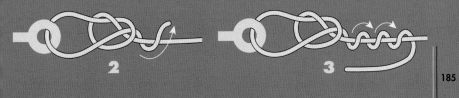

2   **3**

4

5

Duncan loop ❸❸❸❶

This knot forms a sliding loop to attach a fishing line to a lure or reel spool arbor.

Take the tag end around the spool, or through the eye of the lure, and bring it back alongside its own standing part. Then cross both parts of the monofilament with the end to form a loop (1). Pass the end through the loop four or five times (2) to create a series of wrapping turns (3). Pull steadily on the tag end to draw the turns together (4, 5).

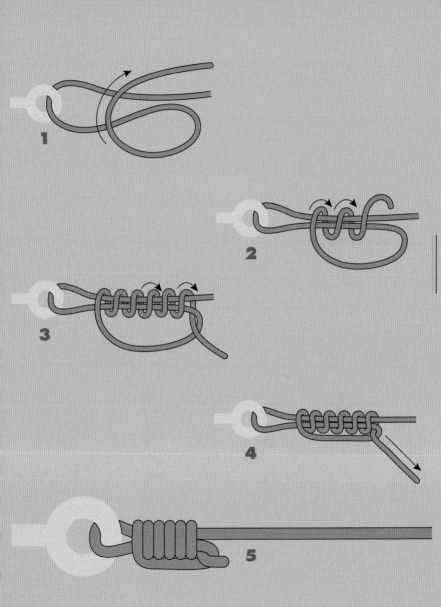

Eugene knot

This knot makes a strong and secure sliding noose for a hook, swivel, or other tackle for a range of line sizes and weights.

Pass the end of the line through the eye or ring and make a long bight parallel to the standing part (1). Wrap this bight three or four times around the standing part (2), then finish off by tucking the tag end through it (3). Tighten the knot and slide it up against the hook or other hardware (4). Cut the end off close to the eye or ring.

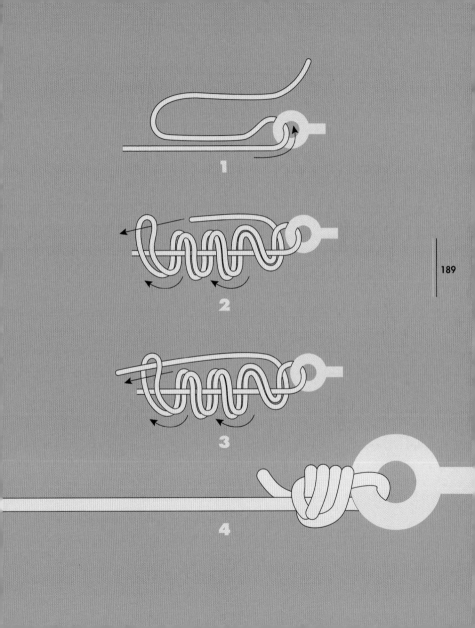

Rapala knot

This knot has—as the name implies—been promoted by the Rapala company for use with its fishing-line products. It is intended for use with lures or flies, its small fixed loop allowing these devices freedom to vibrate, wobble, and dart about in an animated way.

Tie an overhand knot (*see page 292*) several inches or centimeters from the end of the line, then pass the end through the ring or eye (1) and back through the knot in the opposite direction (and from the opposite side) to create a skewed slip knot (2). Wrap the end twice around the standing part of the line (3). Then bring it back, tucking and trapping it, first through the overhand knot (4) and then through the large bight created by the tying process (5). Tighten the knot and trim the tag end off close to it (6).

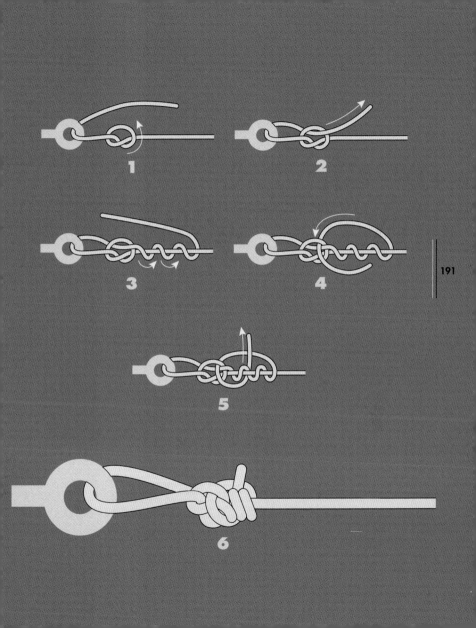

1

2

3

4

5

6

Tegis knot

This knot is a secure way to join two fishing lines. Its sole shortcoming is that the two ends project more or less at right-angles to the line, but they can be trimmed off fairly close to the knot itself.

Make matching bights in the ends of both lines and interlock them, before taking a turn with each working end around its own standing part (1). Tuck both ends, in opposite directions, through the central compartment at the heart of the knot (2). Tug it tight and cut the ends off short (3).

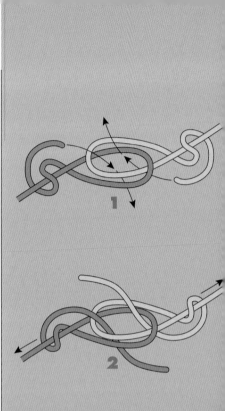

192

Riffle (riffling) hitch

Also called the Portland Creek hitch or the Newfoundland hitch, this knot may be used by fly-fishermen to impart a realistic liveliness to the fly by skimming it across the surface of the water at a 45° angle from the leader. When a fish strikes heavily, the knot may slip off, but—having been tied in the bight—it will fall apart and not remain to weaken the line.

Having attached the fishing line to the eye or ring, pass a loop over the fly's head (1). Add a second loop if desired (2), then pull on the end to tighten the hitch (3).

Arbor knot

This knot (also known as the reel knot) is used to attach fishing line to a spool or reel. It is secure, compact, and because of the slippery nature of monofilament, it will tighten around the reel— all these being requirements of a good reel knot.

Begin by passing the end of your line around the spool of the reel (1). Wrap the working end once around the standing end (2). From behind the wrap, feed the working end through the loop you have just made, forming an overhand around the standing part (3). In the remaining working end, add a simple overhand knot to act as a stopper (4). Moisten and pull on the standing line to tighten— the knots will snug up against each other and the reel (5).

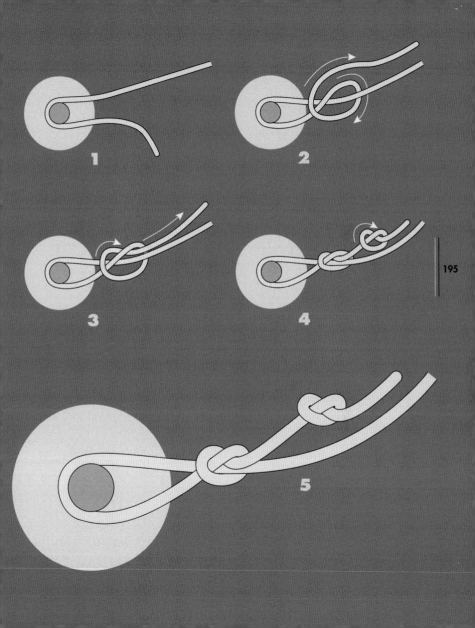

This is identical in layout to the sheet bend (*see page 25*), but replaces the bight in that knot with a pre-formed eye (becket).

Tie a simple overhand or thumb knot as a stopper in the end of the rope (1). Pass it up through the becket and around the back (2), then bring it forward once more to tuck beneath its own standing part (3). Pull on the standing knot to tauten (4).

1

2

3

4

Cat's paw

❸ ⑤ ⑤ ⑤

A secure knot for attaching a line to a hook is the cat's paw, which can be tied in the hand, then slipped onto the end of the hook.

Start with a large bight of line, and fold the top of the bight over onto the standing parts (1) to form two bights. Begin twisting the bights inward toward each other (2). After making at least two complete twists, place the tops of the bights together and position them on the end of the hook (3). Pull the free ends to snug up the twists, and ensure that there is no space in the top of the bights around the hook (4).

1   **2**   **3**   **4**

Halter hitch

Originally employed to tether animals, this sliding noose can be handily applied whenever a quick release would be an advantage.

Make a turn around the anchorage point, then tie an overhand knot (*see page 292*) around the standing part of the line, leaving a drawloop (1, 2, 3). Tuck the end through this loop to prevent its accidental withdrawal (4), and tighten the knot (5). Undo this final tuck and tug on the drawloop to free the hitch.

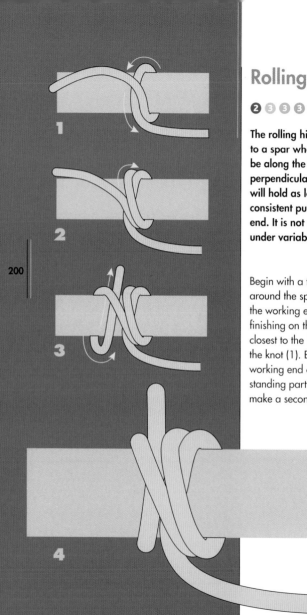

Rolling hitch

The rolling hitch is used to tie to a spar when the pull will be along the length rather than perpendicular to it. This knot will hold as long as there is consistent pull on the standing end. It is not as secure when under variable or shock loading.

Begin with a turn around the spar, with the working end finishing on the side closest to the load on the knot (1). Bring the working end over the standing part, and make a second turn crossing over the first (2). Make a third turn on the opposite side of the standing part, and feed the working end under the turn (3). Pull on the working end to tighten (4).

Slipped rolling hitch

❺ ❸ ❹ ❹

Most hitches tend to be temporary holdfasts. It makes sense, therefore, to consider including a quick-release drawloop, which may also avoid the need to haul a long working end through when tying the knot.

Take the rope or cord end once around the rail, ring, or spar, then make a second and third turn that lie parallel to each other but across over the first turn (1). These two crossing turns must be made on the side of the standing part from which the load will be imposed. Then tuck a bight (not the end) up through beside the first turn and tighten the knot (2, 3). To release the knot, tug on the end.

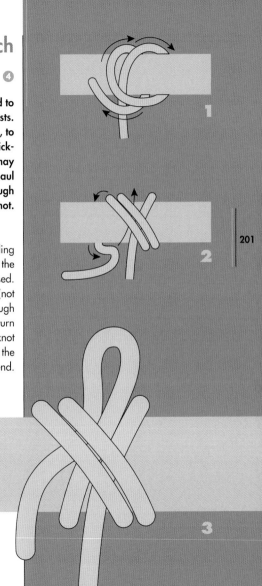

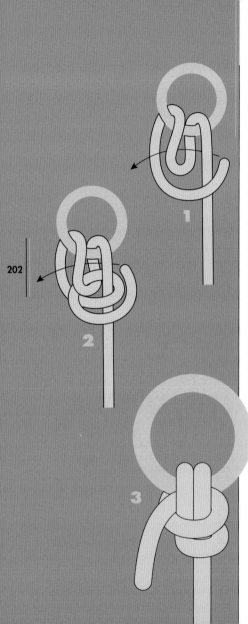

Anchor bend

④ ④ ③ ②

This strong and secure ring hitch (a variant of the anchor hitch, *see page 143*) works in wet or slimy ropes when a round turn and two half hitches may prove less secure. It fastens anchors to their warps, and, because seamen always "bent" a line to a ring, this hitch is known as an anchor bend; but it is equally effective for attaching fishing hooks, lures, and swivels to monofilaments and braids (when it may be called the Nilsson knot, after Harry Nilsson, the Canadian angling author).

Pass the working end through the ring or eye once, then a second time (1). Next, take it around the standing part of the line and tuck it through the round turn, to trap a half hitch (2). Tuck it a second time, alongside the first, then tighten all of the turns (3).

Half blood knot

2 2 4 1

When a secure attachment to an eye is needed using small monofilament, a popular knot is the half blood knot. Generally, blood knots are those that have characteristic wraps going away from the center of the knot. This one is used to tie into a hook, weight, or lure. It is slippery and may release under a heavy load, so should not be used for offshore fishing.

Start by running about 1 ft (30 cm) of line through the lure eye. Wrap the working line around the standing part at least six times (2). Then feed the standing end through the end of the bight next to the eye (3). Moisten the line and pull on the standing and working ends to tighten (4).

1

2

3

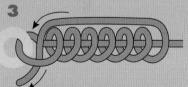

4

Load-releasing hitch ❸ ❸ ❸ ❸

This hitch is designed to be placed into an anchor system, or safety line. It uses many wraps between two carabiners to allow a person to slowly unwrap them and release some of the load, until the weight is on the lowering system again. The X in the knot is important so that the hitch does not release completely, even if it is let go of while unwrapping.

Begin by making a long sling out of webbing with a water knot (*see pages 20–21*), clipping one end into the line to be tensioned and attaching a carabiner to the anchor about 1½ ft (45 cm) away (1). Then make an X in the loop where you want to start the hitch (2), and clip the anchor carabiner carefully into the X, in line with the system (3); it is vital, for safety reasons, to get this step right. Bring the long remaining end of the loop up toward the hitch and through the lowering line's carabiner, then back through the anchor carabiner (4). Start wrapping the remaining webbing around the system to create the friction that will allow you to release a heavy load (5). When you get to the top, use a third carabiner to clip the loose end to the lowering line's carabiner, to finish the hitch (6).

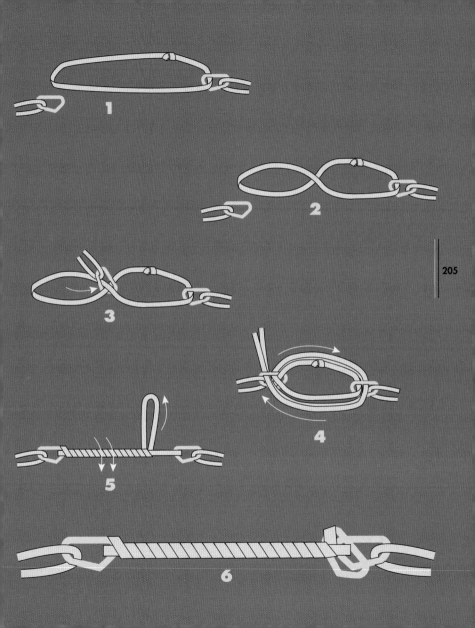

Turle knot

This classic fly-fishing knot attaches an eyed hook to a leader tippet. It was first published in 1941 and a few years later popularized by a Major Turle of Newton Stacey, in Hampshire, England (although he never claimed to have invented it).

Tie an overhand knot (*see page 292*) so that the standing part of the line, upon which the hook has been threaded, is led through it (1, 2). Pass the hook through the loop created by this knot (3) and pull tight up against the eye (4). Snip the end off close to the eye.

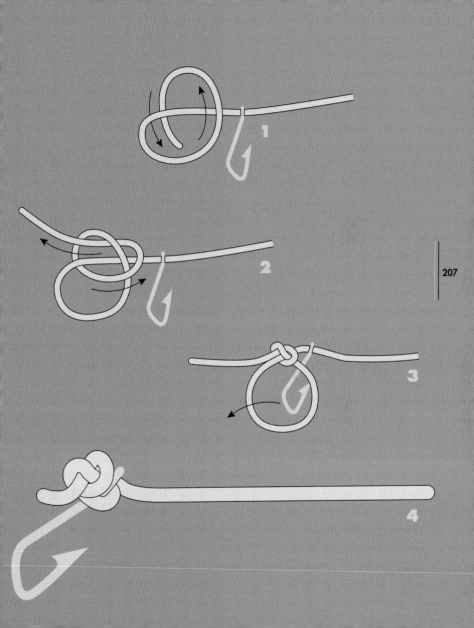

This knot is remarkable for its ability to release extremely freely, with a tug on the free end. Legend has it that unscrupulous types would use this knot to tie off their horses for a quick getaway.

Begin with a bight of rope beneath the spar that you are tying to (1). Place a bight of the standing part through the previous bight (2). Then take a bight of the working end (3) and feed it through the last bight (4). Pull only on the standing part to tighten (5). A tug on the loose working end will quickly release the hitch.

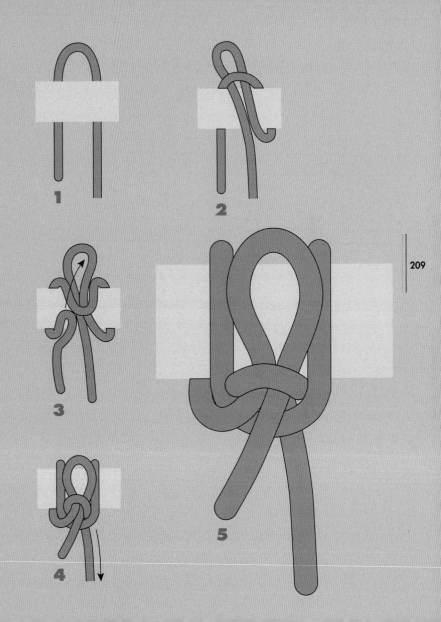

Halyard hitch

Halyards are the strong lines used to raise sails on ships. This hitch was used to fix a line to a rail or post. It is a sturdy hitch that will withstand a varied load, but works best when tied on a surface that has enough friction to hold the rope fast, like a wooden spar.

Begin with two full round turns around the spar, then bring the working end up to the top (1). Pass the working end around behind the standing part, then feed it under all the wraps (2). Bring the working end in front of the knot and pass it under the last wrap only (3). Snug all the wraps close together, and cinch up the working end to tighten (4).

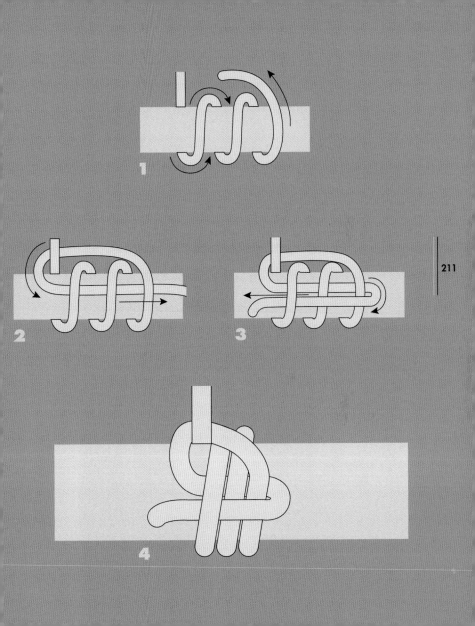

Buntline hitch

This survivor from the days of square-rigged sailing ships is a tenacious little hitch, which will retain its grip despite being persistently shaken or tugged, but for this reason it is a trifle harder to undo than some other simple hitches. Tying it in flat material transforms it into the common necktie knot for men, traditionally known as the four-in-hand knot.

Pass the working end through a ring or other anchorage, then take it around behind the standing part and back across the front (1). Lead the end around the back a second time (2), return to the front, and tuck it over the standing part, but beneath everything else (3). The result is a sliding noose created by a clove hitch *(see page 150)* that slides along the standing part (4). Simply pull it tight and snug against the ring (5).

213

Slipped buntline hitch ❸ ❹ ❹ ❺

The buntline hitch (*see pages 212–213*) is so secure that it can be awkward to untie. Adding a quick-release drawloop overcomes the difficulty.

Tie the orthodox buntline hitch (1, 2, 3), and then simply turn the working end back alongside itself to finish the knot (4).

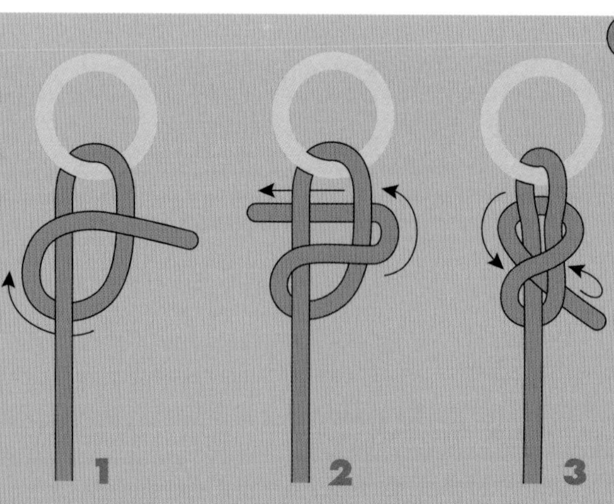

1

2

3

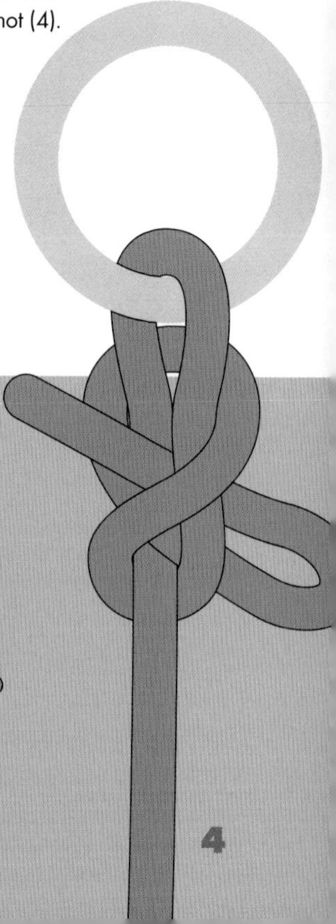

4

Swing hitch

⑤ ⑤ ④ ④

The American marine artist and author Clifford Warren Ashley is generally credited with discovering this strong and secure hitch, although he did not name it. Since it will cope with a load that swings like a pendulum, it acquired its name later. It is easily untied once the load is removed.

215

With the working end of the line, wrap a turn around the supporting rail from back to front, and to the left of the standing part of the rope. Pass it diagonally down across the front, from top left to bottom right (crossing over itself), then back up behind the rail once more (1). Next go down, crossing over the diagonal knot part, and around behind the standing part (from right to left) to emerge at the front once more. Finally, tuck the working end up and under in two places (2). Tug on both the standing part and working end to tighten the resulting hitch (3).

Snuggle hitch

This is another comparative newcomer to the knotting scene, discovered by Owen Nuttall of West Yorkshire, England, and first published in 1987. It is stronger and far more secure than the clove hitch (*see page 150*) and will cope with a right-angled, lengthwise, or variable pull.

Take the working end up and over the rail or spar, from front to back (1). Bring it forward to cross over itself, then take it over and down behind the rail again (2). Crossing over its own standing part (3), take it under the next knot part encountered, then over and down behind the rail once more (4). Coming back up on the right-hand side, take the working end over the first crossing point and tuck it under the second knot part (5). Work the knot snug and tight (6).

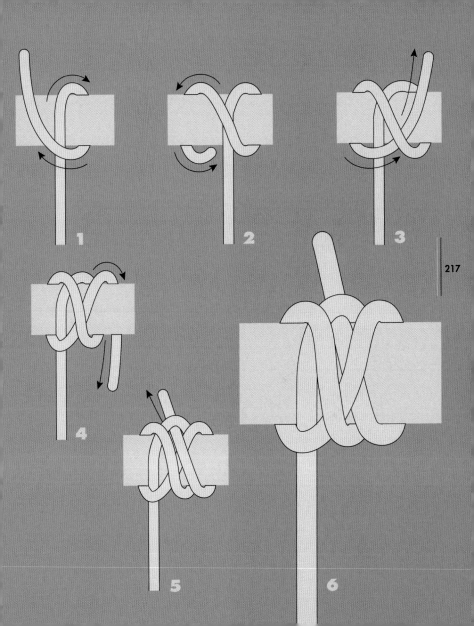

Boom hitch

This handsome hitch has, as its name implies, a boating background. It is a tough and tenacious knot, which will withstand a substantial load from just about any direction, and deserves to be more widely known. Its wrapping and tying sequence (over-over-over-over-and tuck) is easily learned.

Pass the working end over the rail or spar, down behind it, and up in front again, to lie diagonally over its own standing part (1). Go around the rail again, on the left-hand side, and over the diagonal knot part (2). Take the working end over and around the rail again, between the two previously laid upper knot parts, to emerge at the bottom and to the right of the standing part of the line. Make a further diagonal pass, up and over the rail on the left-hand side (3). Finally, come up in front to go over the first knot part encountered and tuck under the next (4). Work all of the knot parts snug and tight (5).

218

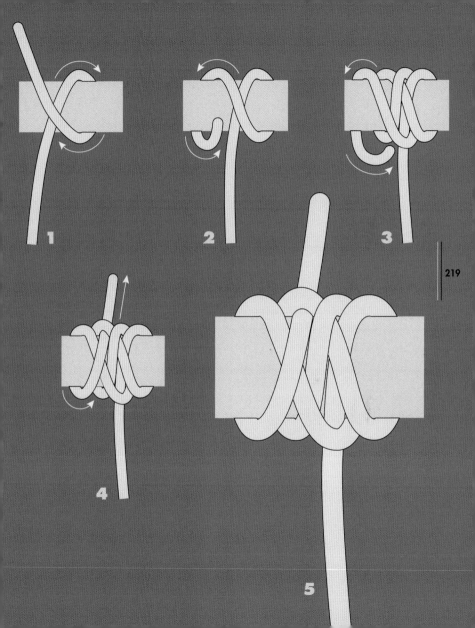

Centauri knot

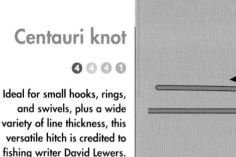

Ideal for small hooks, rings, and swivels, plus a wide variety of line thickness, this versatile hitch is credited to fishing writer David Lewers.

Thread the working end through the eye or ring (1), then make three turns around the standing part of the line, keeping them loosely coiled (2). Bring the end back toward the hook or other bit of tackle, and pass it through the open turns alongside its own standing part (3). Methodically tighten the knot and slide it up snug to the eye or ring on which it is tied, cutting the end off short (4).

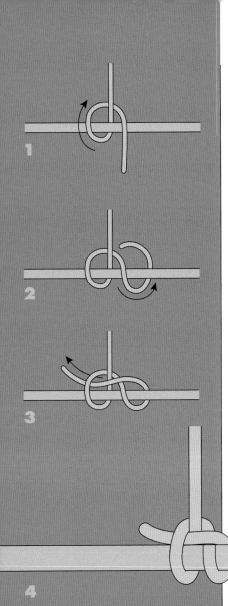

Ossel hitch

● ● ● ●

This is a compact yet tough little hitch, a specialty of the sea-fishing industry, used to attach thick vertical cords at right-angles to the head ropes of drift nets as they are towed underwater. It is equally effective above the waves.

Pass the working end of the line to be attached down behind the rope or spar, then cross the end behind its own standing part (1). Take it down in front once more, then up behind the spar (2). Tuck the working end beneath the initial upward pass (3). Pull on both ends to tighten (4).

Snelling is a versatile form of whipping or seizing that is used, in one form or another, by anglers to attach a fishing line to a spade-ended or eyed hook. It can be as strong as the unknotted line.

Thread the tag end through the eye of the hook and, leaving a large loop, pass it through a second time to lie alongside the hook's shank (1). Using the loop, wrap a series of tight, snug turns around the shank, trapping both parts of the line (2, 3). Pull on the standing part of the line to fully tighten the knot up against the eye (4). Snip the end off close to the eye.

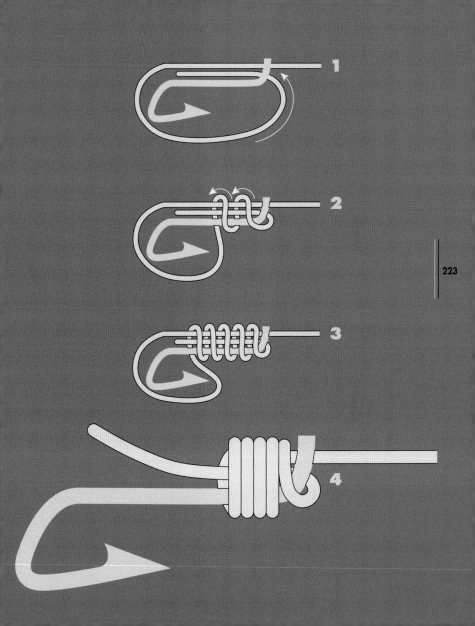

Jansik knot ❺❺❸❶

This knot, often referred to as the Jansik special, ties light lines to a hook, lure, or swivel. Like the trilene knot (*see page 180*), it incorporates two turns around the ring or eye, and it is this feature that makes the Jansik (if carefully tied) almost as strong as the unknotted line.

Pass the working end through the ring or eye of the hook or other bit of tackle (1), then pass it through a second time (2). Place the standing part of the line alongside the two resulting loops (3). Tuck and wrap the end three times around this trio of line parts (4), before kneading and working the lubricated knot snug and tight up against the ring or eye (5). Snip the end off close to the eye.

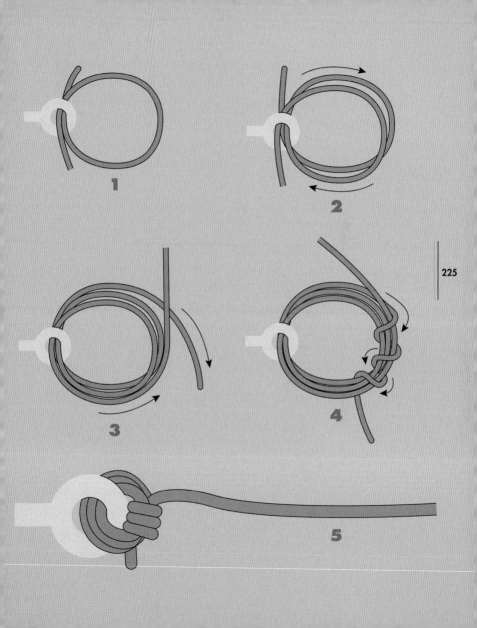

1

2

3

4

5

Offshore swivel knot ❹ ❺ ❹ ❶

Anglers use this strong, chunky ring hitch—which, when tied in cord or rope, is known by boating enthusiasts as a cat's paw—to fix a hook or swivel to a long loop such as the Bimini twist (*see pages 122–123*). There is a neat trick to tying it in the bight.

Push the end of a loop through the eye or ring (1) and pull out a short bight (2). Lift up the hook or swivel and pass it a number of times through the space between the two loops that have been created (3, 4). Pull steadily on both legs of the loop to tighten the knot, at the same time pulling the hook or swivel in the opposite direction, so that the wrapping turns close up and snug down against the hook (5).

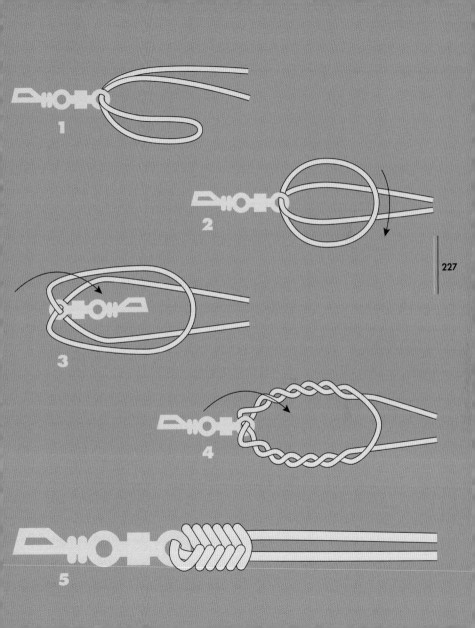

Spider knot | ❹ ❺ ❹ ❶

Some anglers use this strong loop knot instead of the Bimini twist (*see pages 122–123*) because they find it easier to tie in heavy monofilament and braid. It is also known as the thumb loop or trombone loop, and differs from other virtually identical loop knots (known by other names) only in the tying method.

Form a long bight in the end of the line and cast this in an underhand loop (1). Pinch this loop between finger and thumb (2), then wrap a turn around both the thumb and the loop, releasing the forefinger's pressure momentarily to permit the turn to slip into place (3). Repeat the process until five turns have been made (4). Take the remaining bight through the loop, withdraw the thumb, and pull the knot tight (5). Cut off the line close to the knot.

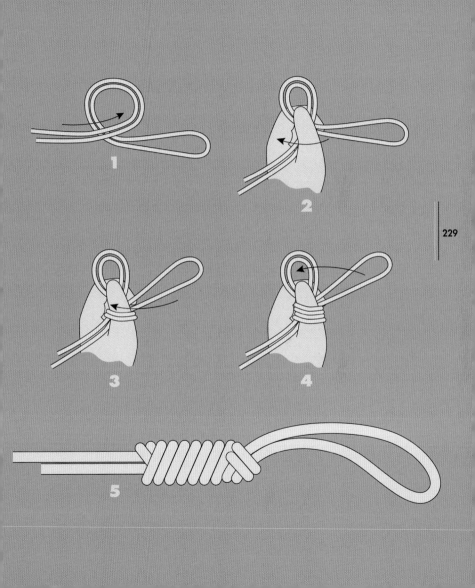

Ring hitch (double-ended)

❸ ❺ ❹ ❹

Not strictly an angling knot, this ingenious hitch will nevertheless link two eyes, rings, or swivels by means of an endless band, provided it can be passed over one of them. At first glance it appears to be an impossible knot, but it is actually quick and simple to tie. Perhaps it was once a medieval harness-makers' trick, but it was rediscovered recently by Joe McNicholas of Pennsylvania.

Pass one end of the sling or strop through one ring and then tuck it down through itself to make a simple ring hitch (1). Take the bight through the second ring, bring it up beneath the crossing loop, and then pass it completely over the first ring (2). Then take the working bight down behind everything to interlock with the initial ring hitch (3). This hitch (4) works equally well (large- or small-scale) in cord, tape, and webbing, or even in a rubber band for luggage labels.

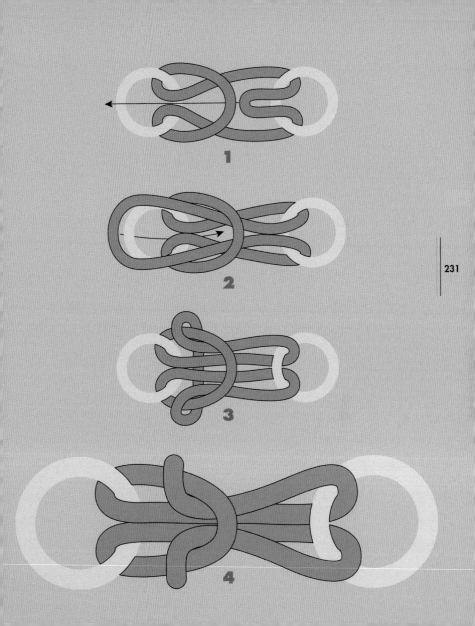

This is a very reliable knot, which can be used to attach most types (and sizes) of line to hooks, sinkers, and swivels.

Pass the end of the line through the eye of the hook or metal item and bring it back alongside the standing part (1). Take the end forward once more and begin a series of wrapping turns, through the loop and enclosing the two line parts (2, 3). Tug the grinner tight (4) and snip off the tag end close to the knot.

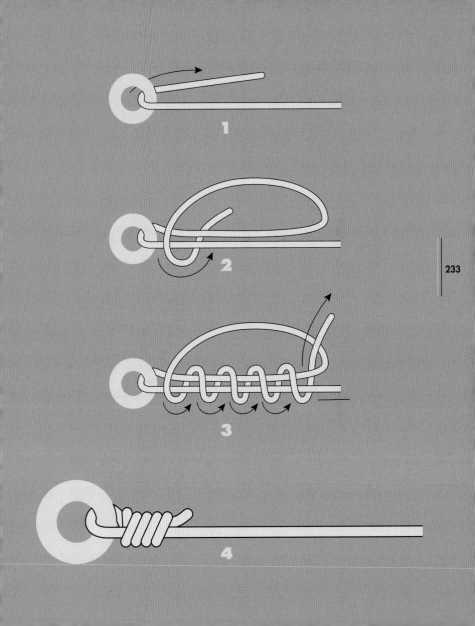

Icicle hitch

The more prosaic name for this knot is an extended pile hitch. It was designed by John Smith of Surrey, England, who first demonstrated its extraordinary resistance to a lengthwise pull in May 1990. What starts out as the working end will ultimately become the loaded one, so allow plenty of length.

Start by making a crossing knot (1) around the rail or spar, then lead the long working end back up and diagonally down across the front, before passing it up behind the spar again (2). Wrap and tuck it at least four or five times around the spar, passing each time beneath the diagonal already created (3). Finally, tuck the active end down beside the inert one (4). Tighten the knot, then tighten it again. Now pull the long end away from the knot, so that the wrapping turns separate and grip over a greater area (5). As long as the couple of turns furthest from the loaded end remain together, the hitch should hold. If they separate, add more wrapping turns.

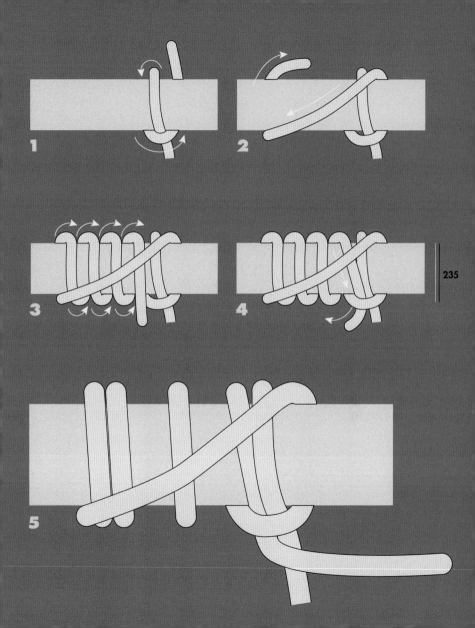

Pole hitch

A couple of these gathering or binding knots will lash together an assortment of long objects—oars and boat hooks, garden tools, tent poles, and the like—and so tame accumulations of bits and pieces that would otherwise be awkward to lug around.

Lay the length of lashing down in an S- or Z-shape and place the objects to be bound on top of it (1). Bring each end of the lashing over the top of the objects and tuck it through the opposite bight (2). Pull upward to tighten the seizing, gathering together the items contained within it, and secure it with a square knot (*see page 10*) (3, 4).

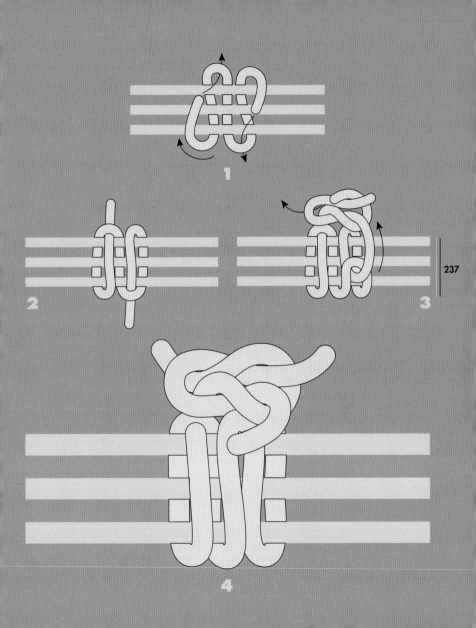

Diamond hitch ❸ ○ ○ ○

There are numerous so-called diamond hitches, all of which are indispensable for tying lumpy loads to pack animals or the roof racks of off-road, four-wheel-drive vehicles. The name comes from the diamond layout at the heart of the knot, which enables the lashing to compensate for any tendency by the load to slip and slide around.

Attach the standing end of the lashing to some fixed midpoint, then pass the working end across the load and around a second anchorage opposite the first one (1). Take the end back to the starting point, entwining it four or six times around the outward leg (2). Lead the end out to one corner, then back and through the central compartment; take it out to the other corner on the same side and back through the center again (3). Repeat this process with the remaining two corners (4). Finally, return the working end to its starting point and tie it off (5).

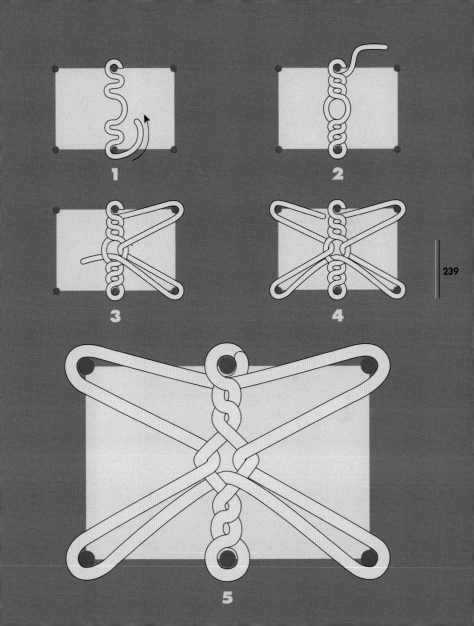

Tensionless anchor

🅢 🄢 🄢 🄢

Another name for this technique might be a "knotless belay." Rigging a climbing rope in this way uses friction around a fixed object, while retaining almost 100 percent of the rope's unknotted strength. It also has the advantage that it can be removed, a turn at a time, while still retaining control over the weight of, say, a disabled climber.

With the working end of the rope, take as many turns as required (but no more) to cope with the load in hand (1). Although this belay is itself knotless, it is vital that the end of the rope should then be secured to a separate belaying point by means of a bowline (*see page 63*) or similar handily tied knot, the end of which should also be backed up (*see page 15*) or stopped (2). The tensionless anchor is then ready for use (3).

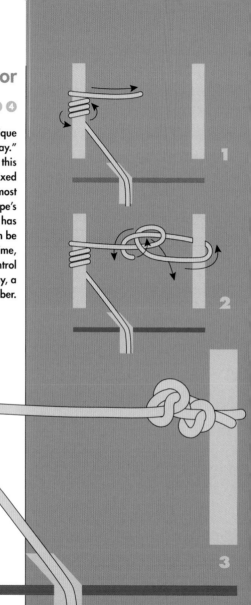

Bill hitch ❸②⑤⑤

Like the single Blackwall hitch (*see page 252*) this minimal hook hitch is only reliable as long as it remains loaded, and it should only be used in rope that is just about thick enough to fill up the mouth of the hook.

Lay the end of the rope in the hook's mouth and then pass it around the neck of the hook (1). Take it outside the bill and, finally, tuck the end of the rope beneath its own standing part (2, 3).

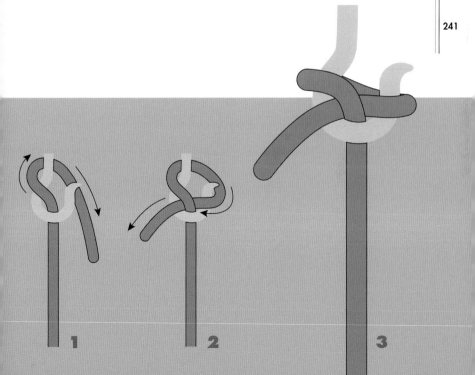

Self-equalizing anchor

When a reliable single belaying point may not exist (for instance, in alpine snow), then a climbing rig can be adapted to share the load equally between two (or more) anchoring points. A bowline on the bight is used for this purpose; so, too, is the Portuguese (sometimes referred to as the French) bowline.

Tie a bowline on the bight (*see pages 68–69*) (1, 2), and then back up or stop the short end to a leg of the most convenient loop (3). As the twin loops of this knot do not readily adjust to any unequal stress or strain between the two anchorage points, a Portuguese bowline (*see pages 76–77*) may be preferable, since its loops are to an extent adjustable (one feeding into the other), although this could conceivably weaken the rope; once again, back up or stop the loose end to a leg on one of the loops. Then spread the load between the two anchorage points (4).

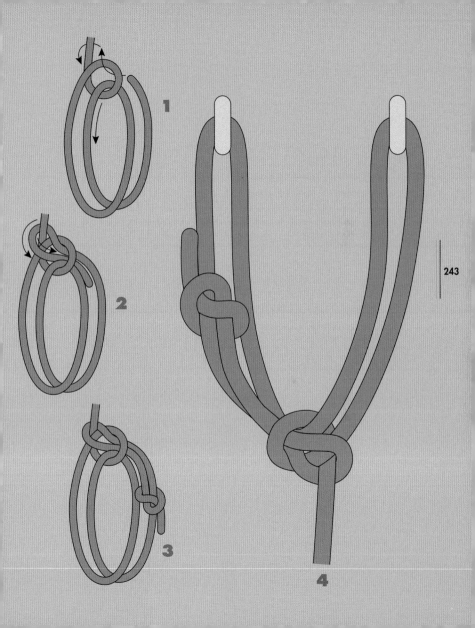

Slide-and-grip hitch (end-loaded)

❺ ❺ ❸ ❹

Tape or webbing comes into its own with this Chinese finger-trap contrivance. To shift it along its foundation, grasp the upper end and pull down. This shortens the overall length and widens the diameter, loosening the hitch's grip. When the load is reapplied, the wrappings lengthen and constrict again. This hitch can withstand a longitudinal pull from a substantial load, and in the absence of any sort of fixture or fitting at the point of attachment, is the proverbial "sky hook."

Locate the webbing's center, then wrap it around the post from back to front, until one leg lies across the other (1). Wrap again, this time from front to back, at the next crossing point going under with the strand that went over before (2). Repeat, alternating the over-under sequence (3), until both legs are almost used up. Tie them together with a water knot (*see pages 20–21*), leaving a small loop to attach the load (4).

244

Slide-and-grip hitch (center-loaded)

See the end-loaded version of this hitch (*page 244*) to obtain the basic idea of how to tie these webbing holdfasts. The powerful grip of this center-loaded sibling withstands a loaded pull from either direction, but may easily be shifted either way by hand, as explained opposite.

Use an endless webbing strop, with the ends sewn together (not knotted). Begin at the top to make the over-under-over wrapping sequence (1, 2, 3). See how a mirror-image plait is created (from the bottom up). Arrange the complete layout so that the two end bights meet in the middle, and secure them with a shackle or carabiner to which the load can be attached (4).

245

1

2

3

4

Cordelette anchor ❺ ❺ ❸ ❸

Climbers who belay and remain static, while safeguarding other climbers who are on the move, must not only keep themselves safe, but also be able to absorb the sudden loading that a slip or fall by someone else might ultimately impose on the belay. One part of the solution is to share the load between several anchorage points; the cordelette does this, as well as providing a point of attachment for the belayed team member.

Thread an endless strop or sling through pre-placed protection devices (1, 2, 3). Pull it into three finger-like bights, and pinch their meeting point together prior to knotting it (4). Tie an overhand knot with the six entwined parts, leaving three projecting loops (5).

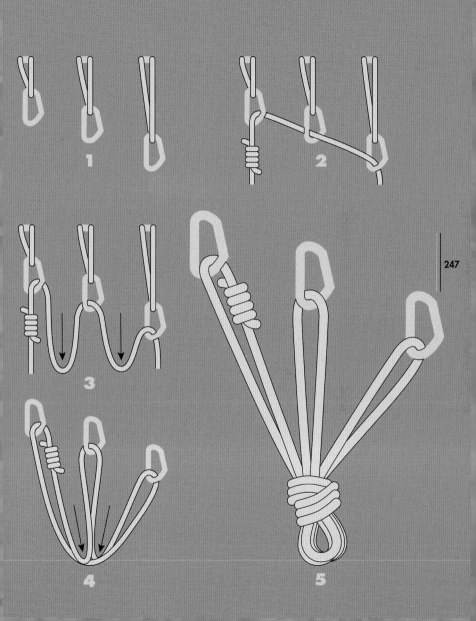

1

2

3

4

5

Scaffold hitch ❸ ❸ ❸ ❸

A pair of these knots can be used, if no purpose-made equipment is available, to suspend an improvised seat for the sort of work undertaken by steeplejacks and tree surgeons. At first glance it seems identical to the pole hitch (*see pages 236–237*), but it has an extra crossing point and an almost sleight-of-hand method of tying.

With the rope's end, make two turns around one end of a plank or scaffold (1, 2). Lift up the rope part furthest from the working end and replace it in the middle of the three strands (3). Then pick up the displaced middle strand and leapfrog it over the remaining two knot parts (4) to pass underneath the plank (5), or whatever is being tied. Finally, pick up both standing part and working end of the rope and knot them together (6)—with, for instance, a stopped bowline.

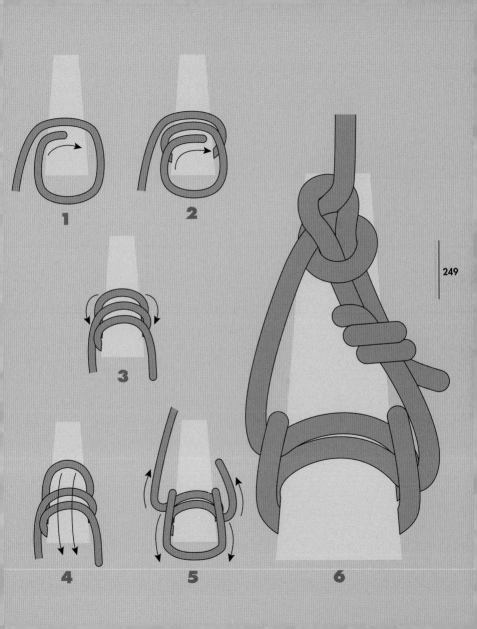

Hammer hitch

3 3 5 5

Use this easily applied hitch
to haul a carpentry hammer
aloft for work up a ladder
or on scaffolding.

Begin by tying a slipped
overhand knot (*see page
293*) in one end of a cord (1,
2). Take the cord around the
hammer's peen (3), and across
its own standing part, so that
the slipped overhand is wedged
securely between the claws of
the hammer (4).

1

2

3

4

Ax hitch | ❸ ④ ⑤ ⑤

Hoisting any sort of heavy implement aloft, or securing it for someone else, requires a knot that will not drop its load on those standing underneath. This hitch also prevents long-handled tools from swinging wildly around.

Tie a simple loop in the end of the line (*see section 2*) and slip it over the handle of the ax (1). Bring the standing part around beneath the axhead and, tying in the bight, add a couple of half hitches (*see page 130*) at intervals along the handle (2, 3). Hoist the ax with the head downward.

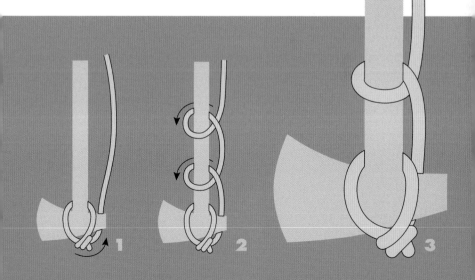

Single
Blackwall hitch

Do not use this hook hitch, which was familiar to riggers in eighteenth-century dockyards, for lifting loads. It is a way of harnessing a hook to pull, drag, or apply tension to something by means of a lanyard, which can be quickly attached and just as readily cast off.

Pass the end of the line through the mouth of the hook and around the back (1). Then tuck it beneath its own standing part (2). Ensure that the end is firmly trapped as the load is applied.

Double Blackwall hitch

This centuries-old method of temporarily attaching a vegetable-fiber rope to the hook of a crane is strong enough as long as the load remains constant, but is obviously insecure. It was a method of hauling taut the standing rigging of sailing ships, but must never be used for hoisting heavy weights or in situations where failure could result in injury, damage, or loss. It is unsuitable for modern synthetic ropes.

Lay one end of the rope within the mouth of the hook, taking the working end around the hook's shank (1), and then around again, tucking it beneath its own standing part (2). This hitch will only hold as long as there is pressure from the standing part on the loose end (3). It is debatable if the second turn (which gives this knot its name) improves or impairs its friction.

253

1

2

3

Bottle sling

Although at least one ancient Greek physician used this knot as a surgical sling and for traction on dislocated joints, it is also an effective way to contrive a collar and two carrying loops for any jug, jar, bottle, or larger container of liquid.

Locate the middle of a length of cord and bend the U-shaped bight down in front of the two standing parts, so that the right-hand loop overlaps the left-hand one (1). Pull out a tongue-like bight and weave it under-over-under-over to emerge at the top of the knot. Take hold of the bight newly formed at the back (or beneath) the knot and pull it down from top to bottom (2). Similarly, pull down the bight at the front of the knot (3). Arrange the result into a circular plaited collar, fit it over the neck of the receptacle, and tighten it. Finally, insert one end of the two cord ends through the single loop, and knot both together securely with a fisherman's knot (*see page 18*) to create twin carrying loops that will always adjust themselves to be the same size (5).

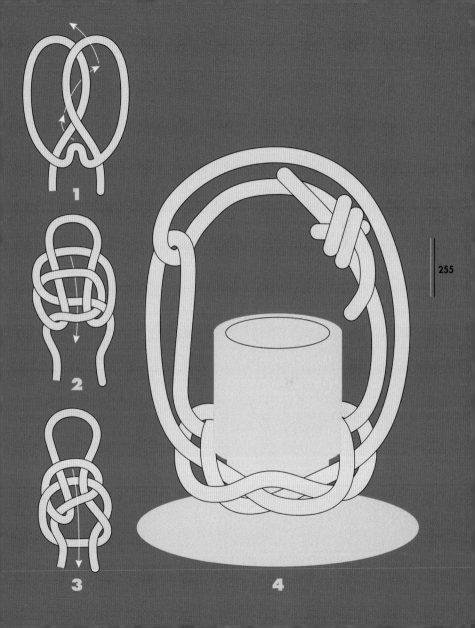

1

2

3

4

Single hook hitch ●●●●

An adaptation of the pile hitch (*see page 171*), this secure hook hitch does not (unlike the single Blackwall hitch) fall apart when relieved of its load. It was first suggested by the respected American knotting author Clifford Warren Ashley in 1944.

Make a bight in the end of the rope and take it through the mouth of the hook (1). Wrap it around the hook's back and loop it over its bill (2). Take care to locate the short end nearest the bill of the hook, as the knot is more reliable that way.

1

2

Ladder hitch

Loops often make useful hitches that can be repeatedly attached and detached without any untying and retying. Use this one to hoist a ladder aloft to wherever it is needed.

Tie a fixed loop—say, a bowline (*see page 63*)—and tuck it up through between the upper two rungs of the ladder (1). Bring the bight down over the top of the ladder legs (2), then simply lift up the standing part of the rope to form this hitch (3).

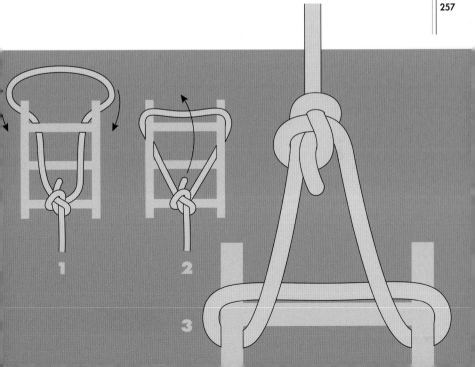

1

2

3

Collared hitch ❺ ❹ ❹ ❹

For thicker anchorage points, this a useful alternative to the ossel hitch (*see page 221*). The standing or loaded part emerges from between a pair of collar-like bights, hence its name. It can be tied in cordage, but is better suited to flat tape or tubular webbing.

Bring the working end down and around the foundation from back to front, then up and behind the standing part (taking care that it lies flat like the collar of a jacket), before going down in front again (1). Pass the end around and up, from front to back, then across in front of the growing knot (2). Then go back down and around once more (3). Viewing the work from the other side, bring the end to the rear (4), and finally tuck it over-under-over (5).

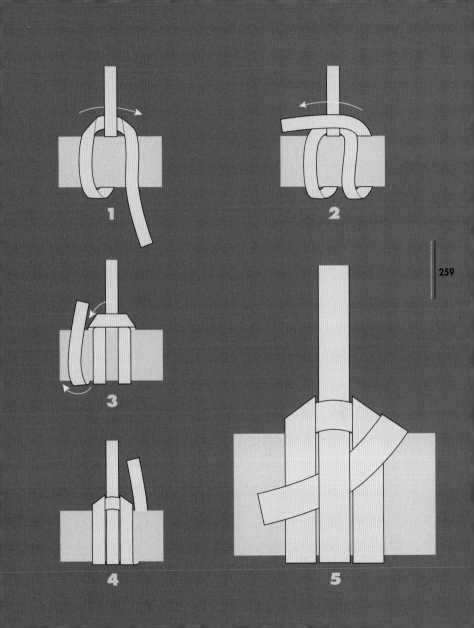

1

2

3

4

5

Snug hitch (reinforced)

5 5 3 3

All knots rely on friction, and this plaited hitch is noticeably more secure than simpler ones.

Pass the working end up behind the rail, ring, or other anchorage point, then down in front and up behind once more, tucking and trapping a small bight beneath the diagonal wrapping turn thus formed (1). Next, take the wrapping turn behind the standing part of the rope (2), to weave it upward in a locking tuck that goes under-over-under three knot parts (3). Systematically work the hitch snug and tight (4).

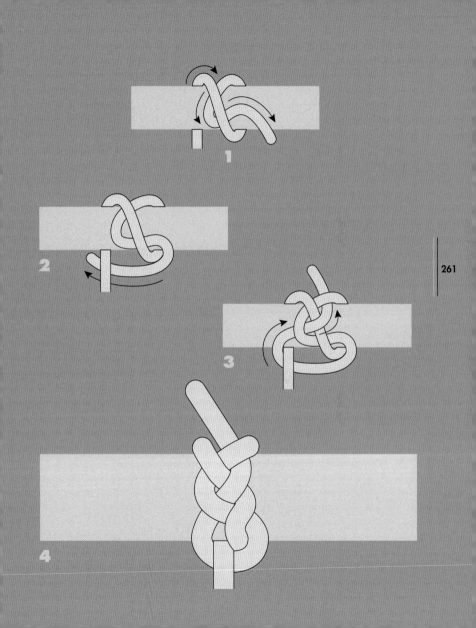

Lashings and coils

A lashing—square, diagonal, or round—is a means of binding two or more crossed or adjacent poles with rope; the same principle is applied to ladders, floors, and planks. A coil is the term used for rope that has been wound into neat circles or loops, either ready for use (the climber's and alpine coils), or for storing (the figure-eight coil).

263

Square lashing

This lashing is used whenever two spars bear upon one another, no matter what the angle (it does not have to be a right-angle). If they tend to spring apart, use a diagonal lashing (*see pages 266–267*).

Tie a clove hitch (*see page 150*) around the vertical spar, directly beneath the horizontal one (1), then "dog" (that is, twist) the end around the standing part of the lashing, for added security. Lead the working end under and around the horizontal spar, thus supporting it, across in front of the vertical spar, then down and around the horizontal one again (2). Follow this initial lead around at least three times—more if the spars or poles are thick, and the lashing is thin—exerting tension every step of the way (3). Change direction and take two or three frapping turns between the poles (4), to grip and further tighten the lashing itself. Tie off with another clove hitch (5), then contrive to tuck the end once or twice through any available space close to the knot (6).

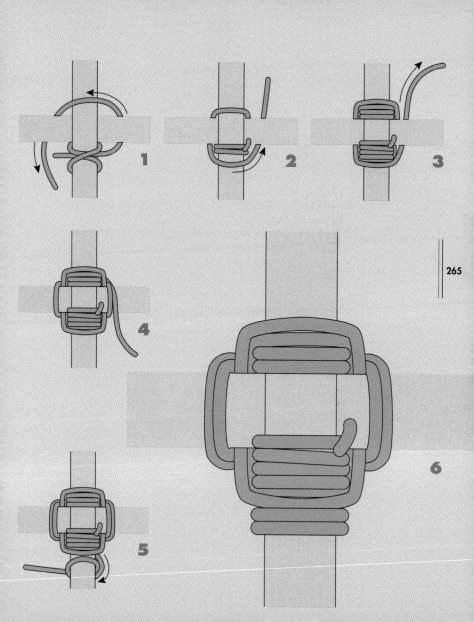

1

2

3

4

5

6

265

Diagonal lashing

This lashing is "diagonal" because it binds and braces poles that cross on a diagonal, whatever their angle of intersection, and that would otherwise tend to spring apart. The diagonal lashing could replace a square lashing (*see pages 264–265*), but a square lashing cannot be used instead of a diagonal one.

Start with a timber hitch (*see page 148*) tied around the two spars and tightened to pull them together (1). Then take three turns around at right-angles to the initial knot (2), and a further three turns at right-angles to these (3). Make a couple of frapping turns, taken between the spars, to further tighten the lashing (4, 5). Finish off with a clove hitch (*see page 150*) (6).

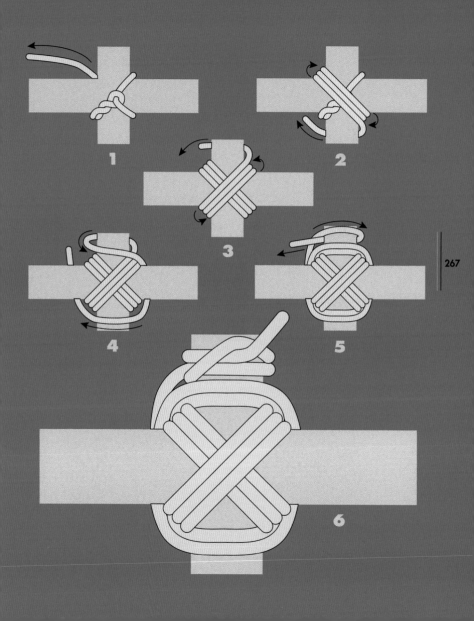

Round lashing

The other name for this seizing is a sheer (or shear) lashing. The name comes from its use by sailors, construction workers, wilderness pioneers, scouts, and guides to lash up a triangular A-frame of poles (known as sheer legs) for rigging a block and tackle. A couple of these lashings will also serve to combine short lengths into longer ones by tying two or more together.

Begin with a clove hitch (*see page 150*) in the standing end around one pole (1). Then take the working end eight or nine times, firmly but not too tightly, around both poles (2). Secure the arrangement with two or three frapping turns taken between the poles, and finish off with a second clove hitch (3). Repeat the process further down the poles (4). Opening the two legs of an A-frame (5) will, of course, tighten a single lashing. Any looseness in a pair of lashings on poles that remain in line with one another can be eliminated only by driving one or more wooden wedges into any available spaces.

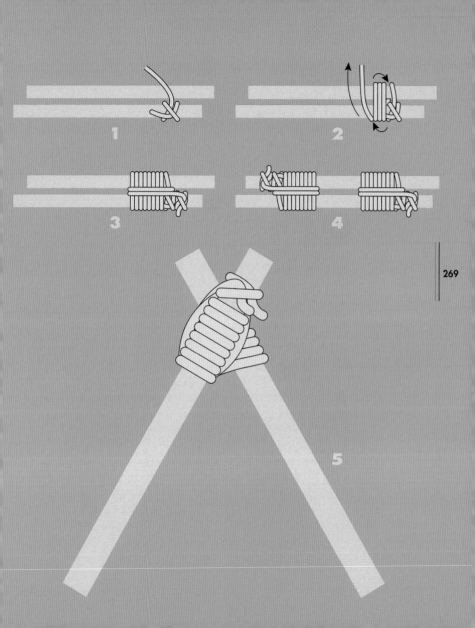

Ladder lashing ❸ ❸ ❸ ❸

Given an ample supply of suitable cordage and bamboo or wooden staves, it would be possible to construct a useful, weight-bearing, ad hoc ladder with this lashing. It could equally well be used to create a robust garden trellis or a makeshift raft.

Take two similar lengths of line and, at the top of each upright or riser, tie a clove hitch (*see pages 150–151*) and reinforce it with a couple of half hitches (*see page 130*) (1). Locate the first transverse spar or rung and wrap the line on each side beneath it for support and tightly around the upright (2). Cross each working end over its own standing part and tie clove hitches on the outer ends of the crosspiece (3, 4). With the working end, lever these knots tight. Repeat as often as required (5).

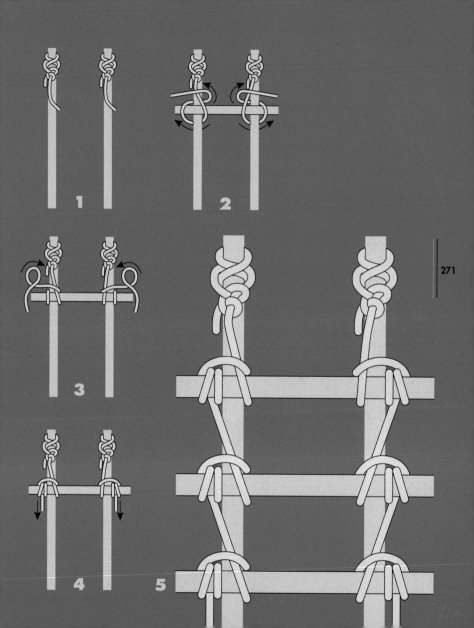

Use this lashing to secure a series of cross-members (for instance, logs or planks) to underlying joists or other supporting beams. In this way anything from a clotheshorse to a log cabin or an ocean-going raft can be created.

Anchor the standing end with a clove hitch (*see page 150*) reinforced by "dogging" (winding) the loose end around the standing part of the lashing (1). Lead the cord over the first cross-member, then down beside the joist or beam, and pull a bight around beneath it and up on the other side (2). Place this bight over the end of the second cross-member, take the working end down the same side (3), then pull another bight up to loop over the end of a third cross-member (4). Repeat the process as necessary, tying off with another clove hitch (5, 6).

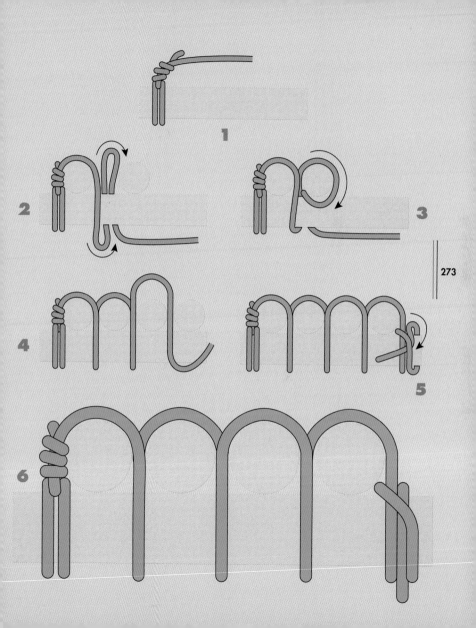

Tripod lashing

A tripod improvised from poles or staves is a useful bit of gear for campers or explorers, and an integral part of many pioneering projects that occupy the energies and initiative of Scout groups.

Lay the three poles down alongside one another and apply the lashing about 12–18 inches (30–45 cm) from the ends. Begin with a clove hitch (*see page 150*), and "dog" (twist) the knot's short end around its standing part (1). Next, interweave the working end over-under-over, back and forth, in a series of racking or figure-eight turns (2, 3). Change direction and add two or three frapping turns between each pair of poles to tighten the lashing (4, 5). Finish off with another clove hitch (6). Tuck the end for added security.

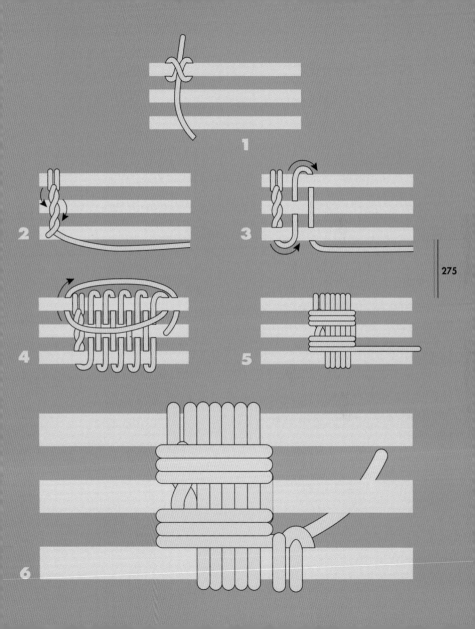

Transom knot ❸ ❸ ❹ ❸

This adaptation of the constrictor knot (*see page 153*) is a neat and minimal way to seize long, thin items at right-angles to one another—for instance, garden trelliswork or lightweight loads (such as canoe paddles) to a car's luggage rack.

Take a short piece of cord and pass the working end in a figure-eight around the two items (1), crossing on top, to enclose both pieces to be seized (2). Lead the end over its own standing part to tuck under-under (3). Tighten the knot by pulling on both ends at once (4).

276

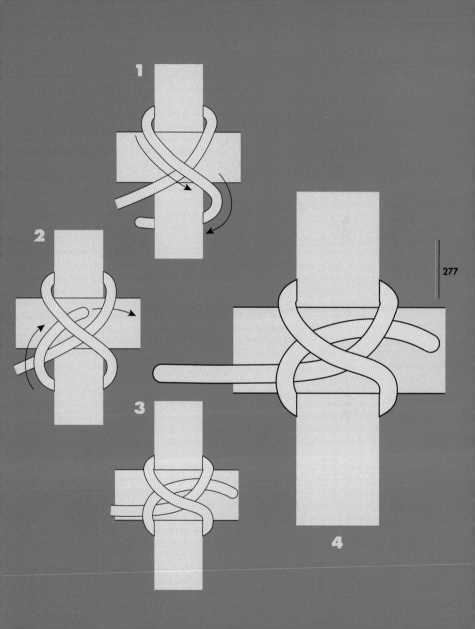

Turk's head

The Turk's head family of knots is the most extensive there is, several thick manuals having been written about them. Tied in suitable material, this basic specimen—with its three parts (or leads) and four overlapping bights at each edge—can serve as an attractive whipping on rope, as a sliding clasp for a neck scarf, a napkin ring, a finger ring, or bracelet, or can seize a hose to a garden faucet. Its uses, like the finished knot, are apparently endless.

Make a turn around the object and cross the working end over the standing part (1). From right to left, go over one strand and under the next (2). Pull one knot segment over the other, as shown, then take the working end left to right over one and under one (3). To complete the knot, bring the working end around and tuck it under the rim of the knot, alongside its own tail (4, 5). By following the original lead, going over where the guide strand goes over (and under where it goes under), the single-ply knot can now be doubled and tripled (6).

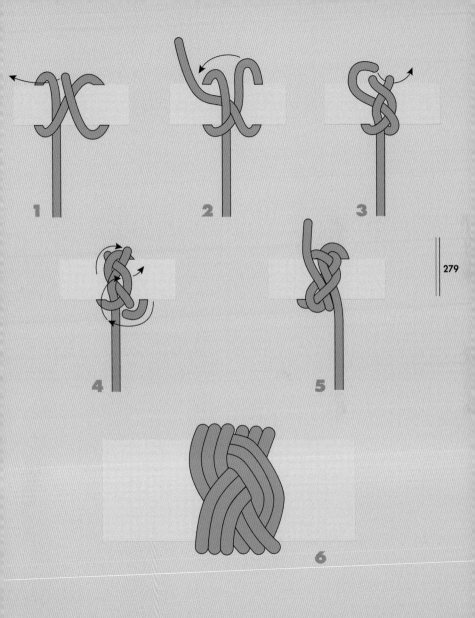

Climber's coil

Enabling any outdoor pioneer to walk, scramble, climb, or descend with both hands free, this way of carrying a climbing rope is also known as a backpack coil.

Roughly measure out three arm-spans of rope and leave this lying on the ground. Drape the remainder, in accordion folds or pleats, across one arm (1). Pick up the unused length of rope and "marry" it to a similar length at the other end (2), then wrap both ends three or four times around the coil, a little above the middle (3). Pull a bight through the top of the coil and tuck both ends through it (4). To carry the coil, take one rope's end over each shoulder (5), crossing them on the chest and passing them around the back, to grip and hold the coil (6). Bring the ends to the front once again and tie them off at the waist with a square knot (*see page 10*).

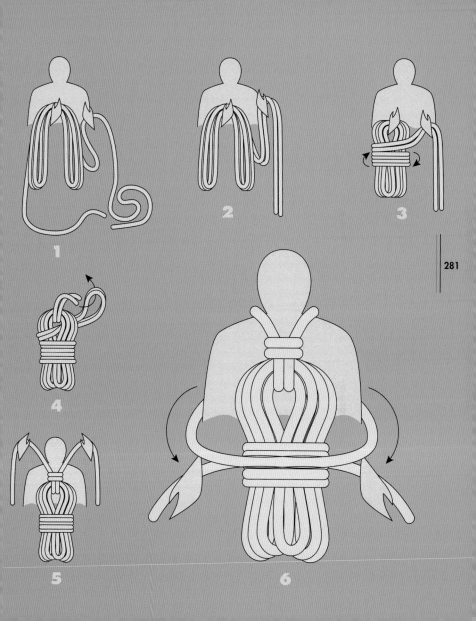

Alpine coil

❺ ❺ ❹ ❹

Some coils are for rope that is to be stored or hung up out of harm's way for a period of time; others are intended to keep a rope handily neat while it is carried, and for imminent use. This coil is one of the latter.

Coil the rope and, having brought both ends together at the top, bend one back to create a bight (1). Then take a series of snug wrapping turns with the other end around it (2). Finally, tuck the working end through what remains of the initial bight, and pull on the other end to trap it securely (3).

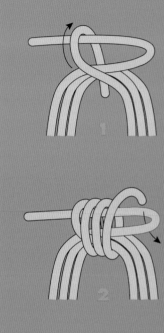

Wrapped coil

❸ ❹ ❸ ❹

A little more time and trouble must be taken to make this coil, but, assuming it will not be needed at a few seconds' notice, the extra wrapping turns keep the rope tangle-free until it is required again.

Coil the rope in the usual way, but tie a reef or square knot (*see page 10*) at the bottom of the coil in both long ends (1). Wrap each end clockwise around and up its own side of the coil (2), until they meet at the top, then tie another reef knot (3). Go over the wrapping turns and work them snug, removing any slack by retying the final reef knot (4).

283

1

2

3

4

Multiple loop ❹ ❹ ❹ ❺

This unusual coil, which can be arranged and carried atop a knapsack, is sometimes referred to as a pack coil.

Make a longer coil than is customary and double it over; then form a small loop in one end (1). Pass this end around behind both legs of the coil (2), bring it to the front once more, and tuck it (from front to back) through its own loop (3).

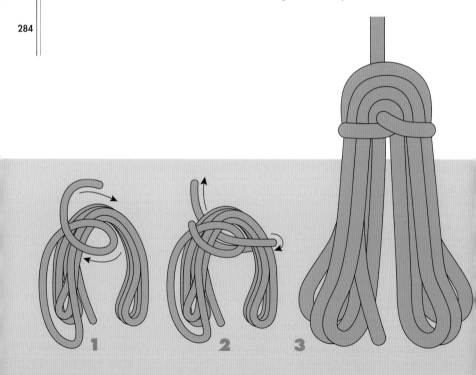

Braid knot

The braid knot resembles a three-strand pigtail braid, but is tied with a single piece of cord. Use it as ornamentation for a whistle, knife, or stopwatch lanyard; tie it around a friend's wrist as a bracelet; or contrive a makeshift handle for a suitcase with it.

Arrange the cord in three parts, with a collar made by two strands around the standing part, then bring the left-hand section over to displace the middle one (1). Next bring the right-hand section over to become the middle part (2), and continue this process (left over to middle, right over to middle). A sloppy mirror-image of the emerging braid will occur at the bottom of the working bight, but pull out the loose end periodically to untangle this (3). When only a small loop remains, make a final locking tuck with the working end (4).

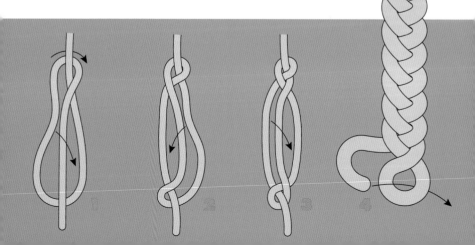

Figure-eight coil ❺❺❹❹

This is a quick and easy way to coil a rope that is to be stored, rather than held ready for immediate use. The name comes from the way the loop is arranged, not the way in which the rope itself is coiled.

Bring both ends of the rope together and coil it, doubled, in a clockwise direction (1). When the bight comes to hand, take it back in a small loop, around behind the coil (2). Then tuck it, front to back, through its own loop (3). Hang the coil up from the smaller loop (4).

Daisy chain

This chain plait (or sinnet, as sailors say) is also referred to as single trumpet or bugle cord, because of its use as an adornment on the uniforms of marching bands. Children enjoy pulling the free end to watch a length of it unravel before their eyes.

Beginning at the standing end of 6–8 ft (2–3 m) of cord, make a slip knot (1). Insert a finger and pull a second bight through the one already formed (2). Repeat the process until all of the cord has been used up, tucking the working end through the last bight to lock all the preceding ones in place (3).

1

2

3

Beaver tail
(double chain plait)

⑤⑤③⑤

This is a bulkier and more good-looking version of the daisy chain, single trumpet, or bugle cord (see page 287); it is, therefore, also referred to as a "double trumpet, or bugle, cord."

Close to what will be the standing end of the cord, form a couple of overhand loops, then pluck a bight from the long working end through both of them (1). Pull another bight through the next two loops (2), and repeat this process as long as cord and enthusiasm last (3).

Remove unwanted slack before drawing out each new bight. Finally, make a locking tuck with what remains of the working end, by pushing it through the two last bights that were made (4).

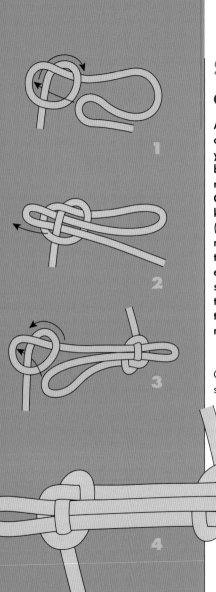

Sheepshank

● ● ● ●

A coil of rope or hank of cord can be expensive, and you should not cut it merely because the job in hand requires less than the full length. Of the various shortening knots known as "sheepshanks" (perhaps because each one resembles a chunky legbone), this is one of the more secure examples and will hold any surplus line not required for the time being. It is yet another of those knots that can—and often must—be tied in the bight.

Grasp the unneeded slack in a loose S- or Z-shape, and in one end form an uncompleted overhand knot (1). Tuck the nearest bight through this layout in an over-under-over sequence (2). Turn the work end-for-end and repeat the process (3). Tighten the resulting twin knots (4).

Stoppers, whippings, and splices

A stopper knot (of which the overhand is the most basic) is generally made to stop rope from passing through a hole and, incidentally, to prevent it from unraveling; a whipping offers another way to prevent fraying. A splice is a permanent means of joining two pieces of rope (the short splice), binding the end (back splice), or making a loop (eye splice).

Overhand ❶⑤⑤❶

The overhand is a very simple stopper knot that has hundreds of applications. It forms the basis for many other knots in this book. Once it is under strain, it is comparatively difficult to untie.

Take the end of the line in your hand and form a loop (1). Then pass the end beneath and through the loop (2). Pull on both ends of the line to tighten the knot (3, 4).

1   **2**   **3**   **4**

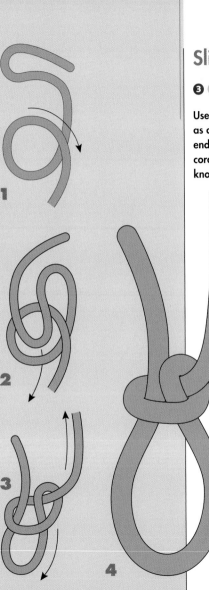

Slipped overhand

❸ ❷ ❺ ❺

Use this quick and simple knot as a temporary stopper in the end of thread, twine, string, or cord. It is merely an overhand knot in which the working end has not been completely pulled through.

Create a loop with the working end beneath the standing part (1). Then make a bight in the end and tuck it down through the loop just formed (2) to serve as a quick-release drawloop (3). This is one of the few knots that may be tightened simply by pulling the two knot parts in opposite directions, in this case the standing part and the anchored leg of the drawloop (4).

Figure eight ❹ ❸ ❷ ❶

This is a useful stopper knot and forms the basis for many other knots in this book. It differs from the overhand in that the ends emerge from the knot parallel to each other, rather than at angles. This is desirable when you need a compact knot that will not catch or tangle with obstructions.

Begin with a clockwise loop of rope, with the working end passing over the standing part (1). Bring the end around the back of the standing part from right to left (2). Then feed the end through the loop you have just made, from top to bottom (3). Pull on the ends to tighten the knot (4).

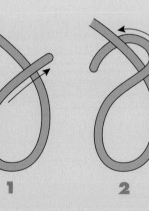

1   **2**   **3**   **4**

Slipped figure eight

This stopper knot is slightly bulkier than a simple overhand or thumb knot; and, although it will not block a bigger hole, the quick-release drawloop makes it easier to undo.

Outline an ampersand [&] with the working end, going first over and then under its own standing part; alternatively, impart a twist to achieve the same shape (1). Then tuck a bight through the upper loop from front to back (2, 3). Pull on both ends and on the loop to tighten the knot (4).

1   2   3   4

Stevedore knot

This is a bulky stopper knot, which is used for making a rope fast through a hole only slightly larger than its diameter.

Begin with a bight, then wrap the working end around the standing part in one complete turn (1). Then make a half turn and bring the working end back up to the top of the knot (2). Take the working end through the end of the bight from front to back (3). Pull on both parts to tighten (4).

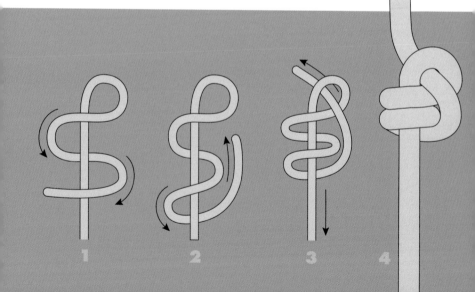

1   2   3   4

Double overhand

This is a beefier knot than the regular overhand (*see page 292*), and is used when more bulk is needed at the end of a line.

Start with a loop in the end of the line, and pass the working end through the loop once, then pass the end through a second time (1). Pull the working and standing ends apart to tighten the knot (2, 3).

1

2

3

Monkey's fist ❺ ❺ ❸ ❸

Any kind of heaving line—whether a "messenger" sent ahead to haul a heavier rope into position, or a rescue lifeline—will fly better and further through the air with this knot on the leading end. It works best with a weighted core inserted (anything from a metal nut to an old golf ball), which will hold the numerous turns neatly in place and add momentum to its flight.

Wrap three vertical coils (1), and then enclose them within three horizontal ones (2, 3), taking care to hold everything in its place. Then change direction again and pass the working end a further three times (once more in a vertical plane, but at right-angles to the original turns) in a series of locking tucks (4). Insert whatever has been chosen as the heavy core. To tighten the knot, start at one end of the knot and—strand by strand, circuit by circuit—systematically pull unwanted slack, a bit at a time, through the knot until it emerges at the other end (5). Lastly, seize (or knot) the loose end to the standing part of the line.

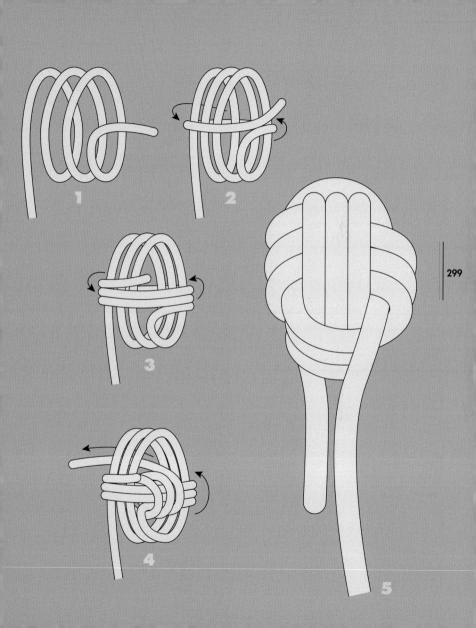

Multifold overhand knot

❺ ❺ ❸ ❶

A cluster of these knots can sometimes be seen adorning the waist ties of nuns and monks, as a reminder that the wearer is bound to his or her vows of poverty, chastity (or celibacy), and obedience. Barrel-shaped knots of this sort also form the basis of other strong and secure knots, although, depending on the material in which they are tied, they may prove hard to untie again. Nevertheless, this is a useful knotting technique to master.

Tie a simple overhand knot (*see page 292*), then tuck the working end two, three, or more extra times (1). Pull both ends gently in opposite directions, allowing the knot to twist and wrap around itself (2). Work it snug and tight (3).

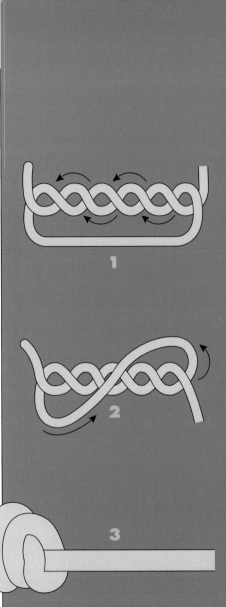

Heaving line knot

When a seaman needed to cast a line to a nearby dock or vessel, he would tie a knot to add weight to the end of the line to make its flight easier. One such knot is the heaving line knot.

Start with a large bight of rope and plenty of excess in the working end. Make a loop around the bight near half its length (1). Continue wrapping the working end around the bight (2) to make the knot as large as you like. Feed the working end through the top of the bight (3). Pull the standing part to draw the bight down onto the working end (4).

1

2

3

4

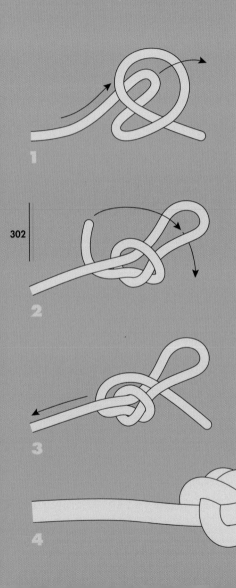

Ashley's stopper

4 **5** **4** **3**

**Clifford W. Ashley, author
of the enormous compilation
of knots and ropework,
The Ashley Book of Knots,
invented this stopper, which
he said gave more bulk with
less rope than other stopper
knots. It can be used to stop
a rope from going through a
hole or eye up to twice
the rope's diameter.**

Start with a loop, with the
working end emerging from
the back of the loop. Pull a
bight from the standing part
through the loop from back to
front (1). Feed the remaining
working end through the bight
(2). Pull on standing end (3)
to tighten the knot (4).

Crown knot ❺❹❹❹

A crown knot forms the basis of a back splice (*see pages 312–313*) in hawser laid rope—that is, three-strand rope; it is also an indispensable technique for ornamental knotting. You can insert a quick crown knot in the end of a cut rope to prevent it from fraying, if whipping twine is not available.

Viewing the rope's end head-on, and assuming that it has the usual right-handed lay, the three strands will appear to rotate counterclockwise (1). Working in this direction, bend one strand over its neighbor, and that second strand over the third one (2). Finally, tuck the third strand down through the first one (3). To tighten a crown knot, tug evenly on each strand in turn (4).

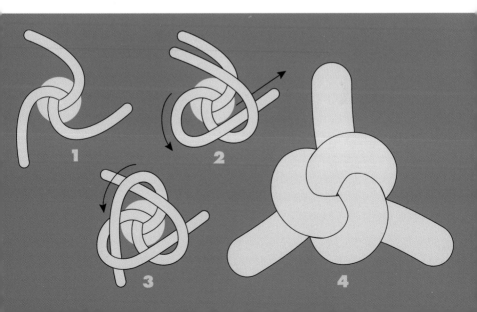

Diamond knot

This ingenious version of what is generally a multistrand lanyard knot— but tied here in a single length of cord—is better known as a knife lanyard knot. Use it to create the retaining loop for a lucky charm, a referee's whistle, an official's stopwatch— or even a knife.

Locate the middle of a piece of cord and make a loop with the working end underneath (1). Pass the other end around it counterclockwise, then under in three places (2, 3). Make a locking tuck over-under-over (4). Still working counterclockwise, take each end in turn around the outside of the nearest standing part and tuck both up through the center of the knot (5). Gently tighten by pulling up on the two ends, while coaxing the entwined knot parts down around the two legs of the remaining loop (6).

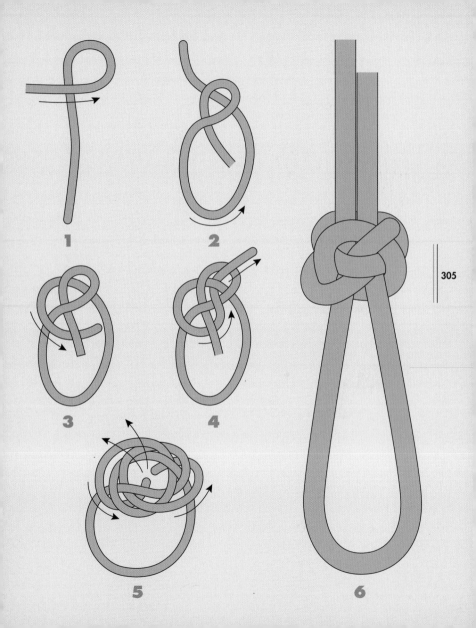

1

2

3

4

5

6

305

❸ ❹ ❸ ❶

Rope is not cheap. So it is good practice to tape or tie it (using a constrictor knot, *see page 153*) on either side of where it is to be cut, to prevent needless fraying and unraveling. This first-aid measure can then be replaced with this traditional whipping.

Lay a narrow bight of whipping twine along the rope (1) and with one end begin to bind a series of wrapping turns (2), traveling toward the rope's end so as to trap the bight in place (3). (For clarity, these turns are shown apart, but they should actually be made firmly alongside one another.) Continue until the whipping is at least as long as the rope is thick, then tuck the working end through the tip of the bight, but leave the final wrapping turn slack (4). Pull steadily but firmly on the unused end of the whipping twine, dragging the working end under and into the wrapping turns; stop when it appears to be halfway (5). Cut off both ends close to the completed whipping (6).

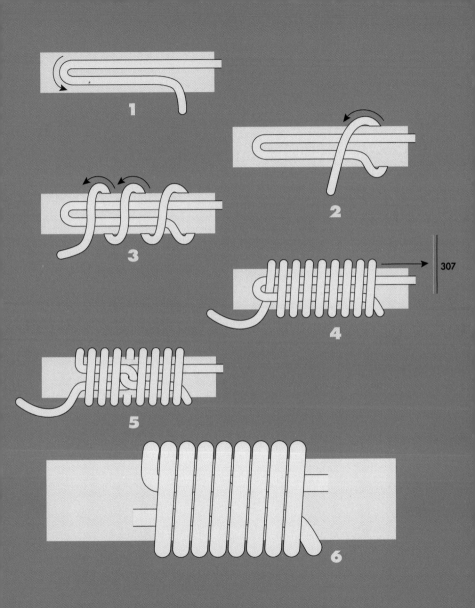

Matthew Walker knot

6 **5** **2** **2**

This classic stopper knot is far from being the only knot named after a person, but it may have been the first, its namesake believed to have been a mid-eighteenth-century master rigger who lived and worked aboard an old hulk moored on the River Wear at Sunderland in northeast England. Tie it in three-strand (hawser-laid) rope. Sailors have their own sleight-of-hand way of forming this tricky knot, but the more methodical method shown here has a better chance of success in fingers unfamiliar with it.

First tie a wall knot, tucking each of the three strands in turn under and up through the next strand around, working counterclockwise (1, 2, 3). Continuing counterclockwise, take each strand around and tuck it up through the next available space (4, 5, 6). Ensure that the trefoil knot layout that results is symmetrical (7), then lift the three strands up and shape the knot into its final, chunky, spiraling form (8). Tighten, a bit at a time, taking care to ensure that the tension on every strand is the same. The ends may either be whipped or taped together for neatness, although this knot is secure enough without that finishing touch.

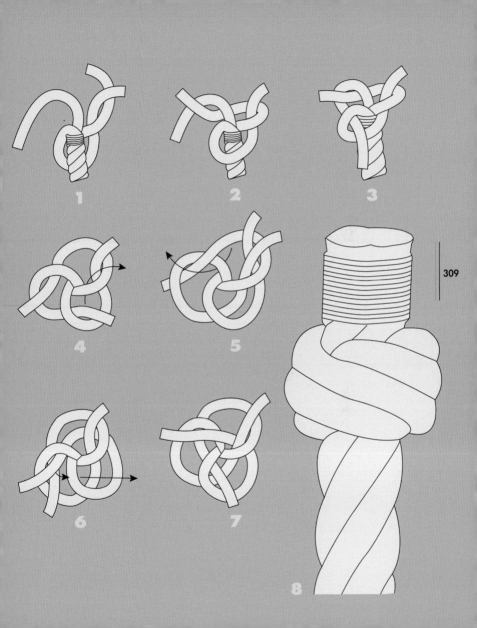

309

Eye splice ❺ ❺ ❸ ❸

This time-honored technique makes a fixed eye of any predetermined size in a three-strand (hawser-laid) rope. Splices are generally stronger than knots in cordage of vegetable-fiber origin (hemp, coir, sisal, etc.) and are preferred for that reason; but in the phenomenally strong synthetic ropes (polyamide, polyester, polypropylene, and others) this may no longer be a critical factor.

Temporarily tie or tape the end of each strand to prevent fraying, then unlay them a short distance, taping the rope at that point to stop further unraveling (1). Keeping the three working ends in order, tuck the middle one beneath a convenient strand in the rope (2). Take the end nearest the rope, pass it over the strand just used, and tuck it beneath the next strand (3). The next step is crucial: lead the end so far unused around to the back of the rope and bend it around to tuck—in the same direction as the previous couple of ends—beneath the only strand unoccupied at that point in the rope (4). Pull this initial trio of tucks snug up against the body of the rope. Continue, tucking all three strands over one, under one, a second time; and tighten by pulling each in turn down (away from the eye), then up (toward the eye). Repeat the process once or twice more (5). It is then usual to roll the splice underfoot before whipping or taping the cut ends to the body of the rope (6).

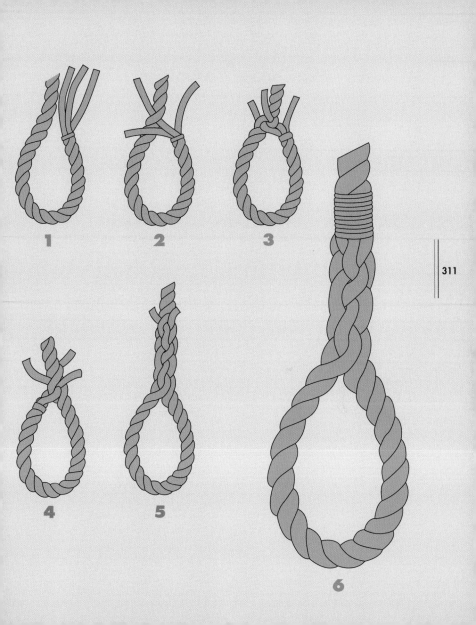

Back splice ❺ ⑤ ❸ ❸

Use this splice instead of a whipping to prevent the three strands of a hawser-laid rope from unraveling, while at the same time creating a good-looking section of six-strand round plait.

Begin with a crown knot (*see page 303*) and pull each strand in turn to tighten it (1). Then select a strand (any one will do) and tuck it, in the opposite direction to the lay of the rope, over the nearest strand and under the next one (2). Repeat this process with another strand, and again with the remaining one (3, 4). Tug each strand in turn downward (away from the crown knot), and then lever it upward (toward the crown), to tighten what has been done so far. Continue, tucking all three strands over one, under one a second time; then tighten as before. Repeat the process at least once or twice more (5). It is then customary to roll the completed splice underfoot before whipping or taping the cut ends to the body of the rope (6).

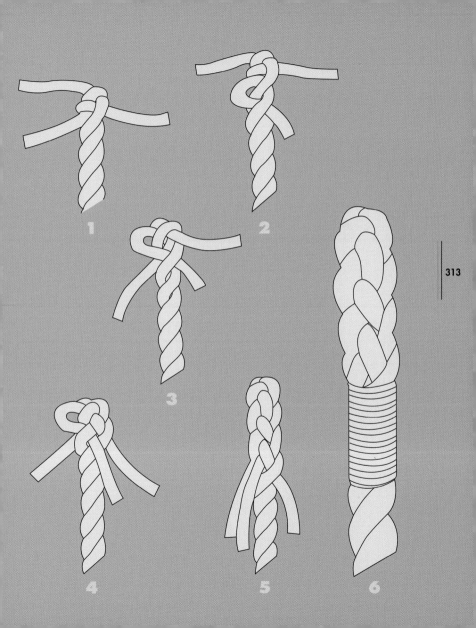

First, learn the back splice (*see pages 312–313*), and then tying the short splice will be easier. Use it to join two similar three-strand (hawser-laid) ropes' ends together, in a way that is both neater and stronger than most knots.

Unlay a short section at the end of each rope, applying a constrictor knot (*see page 153*) or adhesive tape (not shown) to prevent further unraveling. Tape the end of each strand if necessary to prevent them from fraying. Then "marry" the six strands, bringing them together and interlacing them (1). Apply a temporary seizing such as a constrictor knot to keep three strands of one rope against the body of the other rope (2). Tuck each of the free strands in turn over one strand and under the next, then tighten all three, as for the back splice. Repeat the process twice more (3). Loosen the unused three strands (4) and tuck them the same number of times in the opposite direction. Roll them underfoot, and finally tape or whip both sets of ends (5).

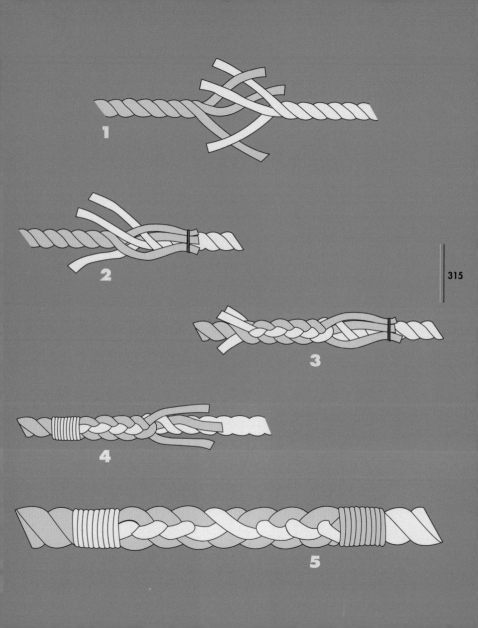

Glossary

arbor: the spindle or shaft at the center of a fishing reel or spool, to which the line is attached

backup: a simple knot (often an overhand) that prevents the main knot from slipping

belay: to anchor a climbing position by means of ropes and fixings

bend: a knot that joins two separate ropes together

bight: a loop formed in rope by folding it back on itself

in the bight: describes a knot tied without using either end of the line

blood knot: a knot with many wrapping turns; it is used especially by anglers and climbers

carabiner: a steel snap-ring with a spring clip or screw gate in one side, used by climbers

cinch: to tighten a knot

cleat: a metal or wooden fitting with two projecting horns or arms, around which rope is fastened

coil: rope that is wound into a neat series of loops or circles, primarily for storage

cordage: a generic term for rope of all sizes and materials

crossing turn: a full circle of rope formed by crossing one part over another

dog: to twist or wind the working end around the standing part

drawloop: a bight or loop created when the working end of the rope is not pulled fully through the knot; it forms a quick-release method of untying the knot

eye: a loop in the end of a line or the opening at the end of a fishing hook through which fishing line is threaded

foundation: a rail, ring, post, spar, or even another rope, around which a line is wrapped and knotted as a form of secure anchorage

frapping turn: an extra turn made to tighten a previous layer of turns

half hitch: a simple knot tied with an end around its own standing part

halyard: a rope that is used to hoist or lower a sail

hawser: a three-stranded rope

heaving line: a light line that is thrown from one person to another; it is often used to pull a heavier rope into place across the intervening distance

hitch: a knot that attaches a line to a ring, rail, or post—or to another line

kernmantel: a rope with a braided sheath enclosing one of several sorts of core yarns

knot: the generic name for rope and cord entanglements; more specifically, anything that is not a bend, a hitch, or is tied in small stuff (such as fishing line)

lanyard: a short length of rope used to fasten or lash an object

lashing: a binding of rope that secures two or more crossed or adjacent poles

lay: the direction (either right- or left-handed) in which the strands of a rope twist

line: a length of rope with a specific function, such as a towline, mooring line, or clothesline

loop: a circle of rope formed by crossing the rope; also a family of knots that may be dropped over an object, threaded through a ring or eye, changed in size or formed of multiple loops

messenger: a light line used to pull heavier rope into position

monofilament: a single synthetic fibre (the smallest element of man-made rope)

noose: a sliding loop

opposite handedness: where two entwined parts of a rope spiral either clockwise or anti-clockwise

overhand: a simple stopper knot, which forms the basis of countless other knots

racking turn: a figure of eight forming part of a series to create a continuous lashing or seizing round two adjacent ropes or spars

round turn: one and a half circles formed by rope round an object

security: the ability of a knot to withstand a steady load and either shaking or intermittent tugs, without coming undone

seize: to bind two ropes or parts of a rope together with twine

shortening: a knot that is used to shorten, temporarily, a long piece of rope

sling: a continuous band of rope or tape; also known as a strop

splice: an interwoven plait that is used to bind the end of a rope, to join two lengths or to make a loop at the end of a rope

standing end: the end of rope, opposite the working end, that is not immediately active in the tying of the knot

stopper: a knot usually made at the end of a rope to prevent it fraying or to stop it passing through a hole

strength: the ability of a knot to withstand a load without breaking

tag end: the working end of a fishing line, particularly once knotted and trimmed

tape: flat woven webbing, which is used by climbers for making slings

tuck: to pass part of a rope underneath another part

turn: to pass a rope right round an object such as a pole or spar

whipping: a knot that binds the end of a rope to prevent it fraying

working end: the end of rope, opposite the standing end, that is being used in the tying of the knot

wrapping turn: any one of a series of such turns, characteristic of 'blood knots', which generally strengthen the knot

Index

319

Further information

The International Guild of Knot Tyers

The IGKT is an association of people—expert and novice, from all walks of life—who share an interest in knots and knotting techniques. The Guild was founded in 1982 and is now a UK registered charity dedicated to "furthering interest in practical, recreational and theoretical aspects of knotting." Publications include the quarterly newsletter *Knotting Matters*. Members are a friendly crowd, with a worldwide membership, one-quarter of which is located within the US.

You can find out more from the Guild's website: www.igkt.net

Geoffrey Budworth was a founder member in 1982 of the International Guild of Knot Tyers and continues to play a leading role on the world's knotting scene. For his expertise in connection with knotted clues found and preserved at scenes of crime he has been called "the father of forensic knotting."

Jason Dalton has spent most of his recreational life outdoors and is a member of the Blue Ridge Mountain Rescue Group (BRMRG). He has taught numerous knot-tying and pioneer skills classes to everyone from rescue workers to Boy Scouts.